THE KITCHEN PANTRY SCIENTIST

MATH FOR KIDS

Fun MATH GAMES AND ACTIVITIES Inspired by AWESOME MATHEMATICIANS, Past and Present

With **20+** ILLUSTRATED BIOGRAPHIES of Amazing Mathematicians from Around the World

REBECCA RAPOPORT and ALLANNA CHUNG

Foreword by
LIZ LEE HEINECKE

QUARRY

Brimming with creative inspiration, how-to projects, and useful information to enrich your everyday life, Quarto.com is a favorite destination for those pursuing their interests and passions.

First Published in 2022 by Quarry Books, an imprint of The Quarto Group,
100 Cummings Center, Suite 265-D, Beverly, MA 01915, USA.
T (978) 282-9590 F (978) 283-2742 Quarto.com

Quarry Books titles are also available at discount for retail, wholesale, promotional, and bulk purchase. For details, contact the Special Sales Manager by email at specialsales@quarto.com or by mail at The Quarto Group, Attn: Special Sales Manager, 100 Cummings Center, Suite 265-D, Beverly, MA 01915, USA.

10 9 8 7 6 5 4 3 2 1

ISBN: 978-0-7603-7311-8

Digital edition published in 2022
eISBN: 978-0-7603-7312-5

Library of Congress Cataloging-in-Publication Data available

Design: Debbie Berne
Page Layout: Megan Jones Design
Cover Illustrations: Kelly Anne Dalton/Lilla Rogers Studio
Cover Photos: Glenn Scott Photography
Illustration of Kitchen Pantry Scientist (top center cover): Mattie Wells
Photography: Glenn Scott Photography and Shutterstock on page 61 (bottom)
Illustration: Kelly Anne Dalton/Lilla Rogers Studio

Printed in Singapore

For everyone who ever disliked or thought they were bad at math.
We hope this book helps you see how beautiful and fun math really is.

And for Ron Rapoport, an amazing father and grandfather,
and the best writing coach ever.

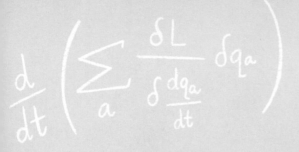

CONTENTS

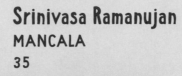

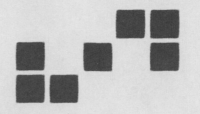

$$\sqrt{1 + 2\sqrt{1 + 3\sqrt{1 + \cdots}}}$$

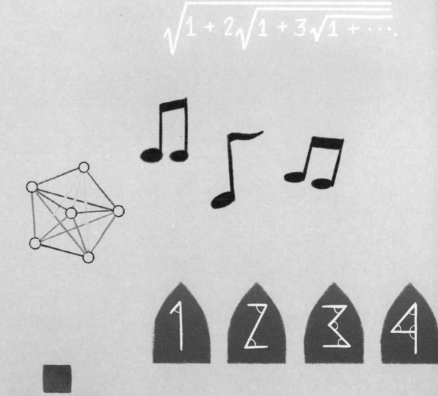

FOREWORD

The Kitchen Pantry Scientist series is designed to make the STEAM disciplines—science, technology, engineering, art, and math—interesting, interactive, and memorable by combining storytelling with hands-on learning. After learning about the life and work of a diverse group of influential figures, readers can explore the concepts they examined through creative experimentation. This interaction between text and tactile experience introduces STEAM concepts in a dynamic new way.

I am thrilled that *Math for Kids* has joined *Chemistry for Kids*, *Biology for Kids*, and *Physics for Kids* as part of this series. Modern science depends on observation and measurement. Without numbers, science as we know it today would not exist.

Math is the language of science, technology, and engineering and can be used to help describe our universe and almost everything in it. In the fields of physics, biology, and chemistry, scientists make assumptions (educated guesses) called hypotheses, which are based on limited observations or evidence. Once a hypothesis is made, it can be tested by experimentation, which involves keeping a record of observations, often using numbers and calculations. In the laboratory, simple math is important for everything from mixing up chemical solutions and counting cells on a microscope slide to deciding whether collected data is significant. Scientists use calculations to make predictions about weather, pandemics, and even the expansion of the universe.

In *The Kitchen Pantry Scientist: Math for Kids*, Rebecca Rapoport and Allanna Chung creatively explore the lives and accomplishments of twenty-two important mathematicians. To spark further exploration, a step-by-step hands-on activity is paired with each math personality.

From Hypatia to Shing-Tung Yau, *Math for Kids* tells the stories of mathematicians throughout history and around the world, accompanied by beautiful illustrations. For example, while learning about "mathemagician" Persi Diaconis, readers will read that a fifty-two-card deck needs to be riffle (standard) shuffled seven times to be considered truly randomized, and then try an astonishing card trick. Projects range from simple to complicated, offering on-ramps for learners of differing interests and abilities. Logic puzzles, paper-folding challenges, and games immerse learners and make the math engaging rather than intimidating.

The Indian mathematician Shakuntala Devi once said, "Many go through life afraid of numbers and upset by numbers. They would rather amble along through life miscounting, miscalculating and, in general, mismanaging their worldly affairs than make friends with numbers." Rapoport and Chung teach us to make friends with numbers.

—Liz Lee Heinecke

INTRODUCTION

Counting has always been an essential part of human existence. From making sure each member of a group was accounted for to portioning out food, math has always been necessary. Math is so important, in fact, that various mathematical ideas were discovered and rediscovered all across the world, sometimes simultaneously, by people who had never met each other. This resulted in different cultures learning different math concepts.

While all ancient civilizations began their math journey with counting, they often expanded their understanding in different directions. Some ancient civilizations, lacking a word for the number zero, had more limited mathematical thinking. Societies that had an understanding of negative numbers could go much further. The ancient Chinese viewed negative numbers as **deficits** and positive numbers as **surpluses**, allowing them to work with both. On the other hand, the ancient Greeks thought the idea of negative numbers was absurd.

Most schools teach math in a straight line: first you learn one concept, which leads you to the next and the next. This often causes children to become discouraged with math. If they have trouble with one concept, they might not want to learn more. However, kids enjoy and thrive in math when they can bring their own creativity into play.

Math is like a tree. You climb the trunk and are met with a fork, two or more options of where to climb next. You can pick one direction at first, then climb back down to explore the others later. The paths continue to split, branching out in every direction. Sometimes, branches will twist around each other, different areas of mathematics arriving at the same beautiful conclusion or building together to form even more possible areas of exploration. Because of all the options, different civilizations explored vastly distinct areas of mathematics.

Math isn't always explored to address a need. Many mathematicians study math simply because it is beautiful. For example, both graph theory and the existence of multiple number systems are integral to the design and function of the Internet. Yet they had been thoroughly studied decades before the invention of the Internet because mathematicians found them beautiful, and this beauty made them curious. At the time these concepts were studied, mathematicians had no idea how important their discoveries would become.

In *The Kitchen Pantry Scientist: Math for Kids*, we explore the lives of twenty-two mathematicians throughout history. Each story describes their lives, work, and accomplishments, alongside setbacks they may have faced. For each mathematician, there is a fun hands-on activity inspired by their work, with a step-by-step guide and accompanying illustrations. Some of the projects are directly inspired by the mathematician's work and others are in a field the mathematician studied. Similar projects are grouped together, so readers may wish to skip around rather than work through the book in order. Readers will learn how to make an alien planet complete with a car with square wheels, solve fun puzzles, play games, do a magic trick, and more! We hope that by showing you how fun and creative math can be, as well as showing you many different branches of the tree of math, you will fall in love with math just like we did!

—Rebecca Rapoport and Allanna Chung

Hypatia

c. 350–370 – March 415

FAMOUS IN HER TIME

Hypatia was incredibly well known and respected as the greatest mathematician and astronomer of her time. She was also her era's leading philosopher. To this day, no other woman has been acknowledged in this way. She was so revered as a great teacher and wise counselor that people traveled from all over the Mediterranean to study under her. Many of her students went on to be famous in that era themselves, yet they continued to seek her counsel through letters or in person. Some of the letters were preserved, which is why we know so much about Hypatia. In fact, she is the first female mathematician historians know much about.

DEDICATED TEACHER

Hypatia taught mathematics, philosophy, and astronomy at the Neoplatonic school in Alexandria, Egypt. At that time, Alexandria was second only to Athens as the cultural and intellectual center of the Greco-Roman world. Her school was extremely well known. In addition to teaching her students, Hypatia often traveled the streets of Alexandria in a chariot to various spots around town where, in scholars' robes, she gave public lectures to large crowds. Hypatia's home was also a major intellectual center of Alexandria.

POLITICALLY POWERFUL

Hypatia was willing to teach anyone, regardless of political or religious affiliation. She advocated tolerance of all and was admired by many diverse people. For much of her life, Hypatia was able to stay above the fray of the political and religious infighting that was going on in the Greco-Roman empire at that time. She was one of very few women who attended political meetings. Many city officials came to her for advice, which meant she had significant political power.

PRESERVING GREEK INTELLECTUAL HERITAGE

In Hypatia's era, mathematics and astronomy were not thought of as separate fields the way they are today. Many scholars in that era spent significant effort preserving and expanding upon classical math/astronomy texts in an effort to preserve their Greek mathematical and astronomical heritage. For example, Hypatia is known for editing Ptolemy's *Almagest*, an extremely important math/astronomy text that described the geometry of planetary motion as it was understood in that era. The Earth-centric view of the universe in the *Almagest* held for 1,200 years! She also edited Apollonius's *Conics*, another highly influential Greek text about the geometry of conic sections. It includes the definitions of ellipse, parabola, and hyperbola that we still use today. Some of Hypatia's commentary on Diophantus's *Arithmetica*, a third famous text, survives to this day. She invented an improved method for the long division algorithms used in various astronomy calculations. In addition to revising and improving Ptolemy's *Almagest*, she created her own *Astronomical Tables*. Hypatia's math books, which were devised to assist teaching, were still popular more than a century after her death.

LEGACY

Hypatia is believed to be the inspiration for Saint Catherine of Alexandria, who was known for being wise and highly educated. Hypatia has appeared as a character in various historical fiction books and movies. In the twentieth century, Hypatia became an icon for women's rights.

SQUARE WHEELS

You may have heard a joke about how useless square wheels are. Hypatia loved to use geometry in useful ways, so in this project we're going to make a square-wheeled car that works just fine!

MATERIALS

- Tape
- 10 or more toilet paper rolls
- 1 long thin piece of cardboard, at least 18 by 5 inches (45.7 by 12.7 cm)
- Craft knife or scissors
- If using craft knife: Cutting mat or other safe surface on which to use craft knife
- 1 small piece of cardboard, at least 4.25 by 2 inches (10.8 by 2.5 cm)
- 1 straw at least 4 inches (10.2 cm) long
- 4 small pieces of cardboard, at least 2 by 2 inches (5.1 by 5.1 cm)
- Ruler
- Pencil
- 1 wood skewer, at least 6 inches (15.2 cm) long (or two 3-inch [7.6 cm] skewers)
- Glue, preferably from a hot glue gun

NOTE: This project assumes you use standard American toilet paper rolls that are approximately 4½ inches (11.4 cm) wide and approximately 1¹¹⁄₁₆ inches (4.3 cm) in diameter. Ignore the rest of this note if you are using standard American toilet paper rolls. If your toilet paper rolls are a different size, measure their diameter (the distance across the widest part of the circular part of the tube) and multiply by 1.2. Use that number for the length of the sides of your square wheels (step 4).

Fig. 7. Put the car on the road and drive!

DIRECTIONS

1 First make the road for the car. Tape at least ten toilet paper rolls to the long piece of cardboard so the rolls are right next to each other. You may wish to trim the long piece of cardboard so it is the same width as the length of the toilet paper rolls. *Fig. 1.*

2 Cut a 4.25- by 2-inch (10.8 by 2.5 cm) piece of cardboard to use as the body of your car.

3 Cut two 2-inch (5.1 cm) pieces of straw and tape one to each end of the car's body. *Fig. 2.*

4 Cut four 2- by 2-inch (5.1 by 5.1 cm) square wheels. *Fig. 3.*

5 With a ruler and pencil, draw diagonals on each square wheel to precisely find the center. Carefully use a craft knife or sharp scissors to poke a small hole at the center of each wheel. *Fig. 4.*

6 Cut two pieces of skewer, each at least 3 inches (7.6 cm) long.

7 Poke a skewer through the hole you previously poked in the center of one of the wheels.

8 Pass the skewer through one of the straws, then attach another wheel on the other side. *Fig. 5.*

9 Repeat for the other skewer and the other two wheels.

10 Check that the wheels are aligned with each other so the flat parts lie flat at the same time. *Fig. 6.*

11 Make sure each pair of wheels spins freely in its straw.

12 If your wheels spin separately from each other on a skewer, put a dab of hot glue in each of the holes where the skewer goes through the center of the wheel. Make sure the wheels stay aligned!

13 Now comes the fun part! Put your car on the road and drive! *Fig. 7.*

Fig. 1. Tape the toilet paper rolls to the cardboard.

Fig. 2. Tape the straw pieces to the car's body.

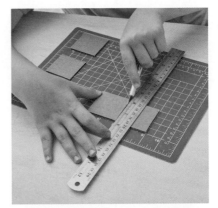

Fig. 3. Cut four 2- by 2-inch (5.1 by 5.1 cm) square wheels.

Fig. 4. Poke a small hole in the center of each wheel.

Fig. 5. Pass the skewer through the straw, then attach the other wheel.

Fig. 6. Check that the wheels are aligned with each other.

BONUS LEVEL

Before you go on to the next section, think about this question: Did you notice that the car drives smoothly? You may have guessed that the car would go up and down as it rode over the peaks and valleys of the road. But the car stayed at the same height the whole time. Can you figure out why it was a smooth ride?

THE MATH IN THE FUN

As the car moves along the road, the corners of the wheels go in the valleys and the flat parts of the wheels go over the peaks of the road. The wheel axles stay the same height and the ride is smooth!

Actually, the toilet paper rolls aren't making a perfectly smooth ride, but they're pretty close. To get a truly smooth ride, our road would have to be made of **catenary curves**. Catenary curves are used in engineering because they make the strongest arches. Apparently, Thomas Jefferson invented the word to describe the arches used to build some bridges. The Gateway Arch in St. Louis, Missouri, is often given as an example of a catenary curve, but it's actually not! It is pretty close, though.

Some historians believe this concept was used by the Egyptians when they made the pyramids. The idea is that the Egyptians built catenary tracks leading up to the pyramids so they could roll the stone blocks right up to where they were needed!

Maryam Mirzakhani

May 12, 1977 – July 14, 2017

WANTED TO BE A WRITER

When she was growing up, Maryam Mirzakhani wanted to become a writer. She went to a middle school that was part of Iran's National Organization for the Development of Exceptional Talents and did not do very well in her first math class there. She was so discouraged that she wondered whether she was any good at math. Luckily, the next year she had a better experience. By high school, Maryam was so interested in math that she convinced the principal of her all-girls school that they should have the same math problem-solving classes as the boys' high school. Those classes paid off when Maryam won a gold medal in the International Math Olympiad her junior year, missing only one point. The next year, Maryam got that last point, taking gold again with a perfect score.

EARLY SUCCESS

Maryam moved to the United States and got a PhD in math from Harvard University. Her thesis was so impressive that it turned into three significant papers in three of the biggest math journals. After earning her doctorate, she spent a little time as a professor at Princeton University before moving to Stanford University in California, where she stayed for the rest of her career.

UNIQUE WORK METHODS

The *Stanford News* reported that Maryam preferred to work by drawing images related to her research on large sheets of paper, writing formulas around the edges of her sketches: "Her young daughter described her mother at work as 'painting.'" Maryam liked to tackle problems in areas usually considered separate. She said, "I like crossing the imaginary boundaries people set up between different fields. . . . There are lots of tools, and you don't know which one would work. It's about being optimistic and trying to connect things." Maryam didn't just solve major problems. She also developed new tools to help other people solve different problems.

FIELDS MEDAL

In 2014, Dr. Maryam Mirzakhani became not only the first woman to win the Fields Medal but also the first Iranian. The Fields Medal is the highest award in mathematics—many people think of it as the Nobel Prize in math. When Maryam won, some Iranian newspapers doctored her picture to show her with a hijab (head scarf) because publishing a picture of a woman not wearing a hijab is taboo in Iran. Other papers published her picture without a hijab. The president of Iran caused some controversy as well when he congratulated Maryam on Twitter and included a photo of her without a head scarf.

EARLY DEATH

Tragically, Maryam died at age forty of breast cancer. News of her death made the front page of newspapers around the world. About a year after her death, the Women's Committee of the Iranian Mathematical Society proposed that her birthday—May 12—be celebrated as Women in Mathematics Day. The proposal was approved and the first Women in Mathematics Day was observed on May 12, 2019.

STRAIGHT EDGE, CURVED SLOT

One of the fields Maryam Mirzakhani studied was hyperbolic geometry. Let's learn what a hyperbola is and use one to pass a straight pencil through a curved slot!

MATERIALS

- Hyperbolic Slot template from the back of the book (it can also be downloaded from www.mathlabforkids.com and https://quarto.com/files/MathForKids)
- Tape
- A piece of cardboard at least 9 inches (23 cm) tall and 4 inches (10.2 cm) wide
- Scissors (optional)
- Pencil or pen for writing
- Craft knife or box cutter
- Cutting mat, large piece of cardboard, or other safe cutting surface
- Rubber band
- Number 2 pencil to use as the stick that goes through the slot

SAFETY TIPS AND HINTS

- The steps that involve a craft knife/box cutter should be supervised or performed by an adult.
- An adult should decide what surface is suitable for cutting.

DIRECTIONS

1 Make a copy of the Hyperbolic Slot template from the back of the book. It can also be downloaded from www.mathlabforkids.com and https://quarto.com/files/MathForKids.

Fig. 1. Cut the slot in the cardboard.

2 Tape the Hyperbolic Slot template to the 9- by 4-inch (23 by 10.2 cm) piece of cardboard or cut it out with scissors and trace it on the cardboard.

3 Use the craft knife and cutting mat to cut the hyperbola-shaped slot from the template in the cardboard. *Fig. 1.*

4 Decide which side will be the "back" of your slot. You may not care, but if there is writing on one side, that should probably be your back.

5 Lay the rubber band across the middle of the "back" side of the slot.

6 Lay the pencil on top of the rubber band.

7 Line up the middle of the pencil with the middle of the rubber band.

8 Tape one side of the rubber band on one side of the slot. *Fig. 2.*

Fig. 2. Tape one side of the rubber band.

Fig. 3. Wrap the rubber band around the pencil.

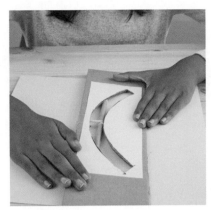

Fig. 4. Flip the slot over so the pencil is behind.

Fig. 5. Pass the pencil top through the curve.

Fig. 6. Pass the pencil bottom through the curve.

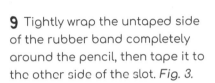

9 Tightly wrap the untaped side of the rubber band completely around the pencil, then tape it to the other side of the slot. *Fig. 3.*

10 Flip your slot back over to the front. *Fig. 4.*

11 Rotate the pencil so it traces the shape of the curved slot, passing first the top, then the bottom, through the curve. For extra guidance, there's a video of this step at www.mathlabforkids.com. *Fig. 5* and *Fig. 6.*

12 Amazing! Your straight pencil passed through a curved slot!

THE MATH IN THE FUN

The three-dimensional hourglass shape the pencil sweeps out as it rotates through the space is called a **hyperboloid**. The purple of the image (below) is an example of a hyperboloid.

The straight pencil can pass through the curved slot because as it rotates through the slot, it moves through a cross-section of the hyperboloid (the dotted lines in the image). That two-dimensional cross-section is called a **hyperbola**.

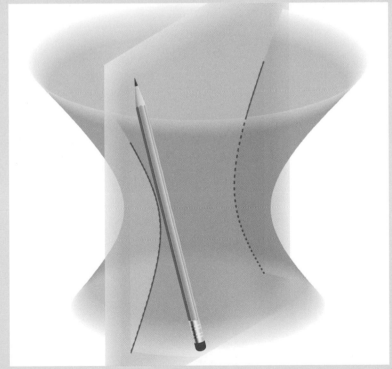

Hyperboloid and hyperbola cross-sections.

J. Ernest Wilkins Jr.

November 27, 1923 – May 1, 2011

EARLY BRILLIANCE

When J. Ernest Wilkins Jr. was thirteen, he became the youngest student ever admitted to the University of Chicago. He got his PhD only a few days after he turned nineteen. Newspapers around the United States celebrated him as a genius! Ernest scored in the top ten in the Putnam Competition, a math contest for college students all over North America. He was also the University of Chicago table tennis (ping-pong) champion three times.

THE MANHATTAN PROJECT

Ernest was a professor at what is now called Tuskegee University until he returned to the University of Chicago to work on the Manhattan Project during World War II. Although he worked in the lab that created the materials needed for a nuclear bomb, Ernest didn't realize that was the goal of the Manhattan Project. He thought they were doing nuclear energy research. Some of his research on nuclear-reactor physics resulted in what is now known as the Wilkins effect. He also worked with future Nobel Prize winner Eugene Wigner on what is now known as the Wigner-Wilkins spectrum, estimating neutron energy distribution inside nuclear reactors. They also developed mathematical models for neutron absorption. When Ernest's team was transferred from the University of Chicago to Tennessee, he refused to move with them because as an African American, he wouldn't be treated the same as the white members of his team in Tennessee. Edward Teller, "the father of the hydrogen bomb," personally made sure that Ernest found a new post where he could continue to help the war effort.

WORK IN UNIVERSITY, GOVERNMENT, AND BUSINESS

Ernest had an incredibly impressive career across six decades, working not only as a professor but also in government and business. He earned two more degrees and rose to manager of research and development at United Nuclear Corporation. He co-founded a company that designed and developed nuclear reactors to make electricity. Ernest was a distinguished (senior) professor at Howard University, where he started a math PhD program. This made Howard University the first traditionally Black university to have such a program. He was also a senior staff member at the Argonne National Laboratory, which researches and develops peaceful uses of nuclear energy.

AWARDS AND HONORS

Dr. Ernest Wilkins Jr. received many awards and honors— he was president of the American Nuclear Society, inducted into the National Academy of Engineering, and awarded the Outstanding Civilian Service Medal by the U.S. Army. He was elected as a fellow to the American Association for the Advancement of Science and the American Nuclear Society. He was also an honorary life member of the National Association of Mathematicians.

INFLUENCE IN TODAY'S WORLD

Ernest's work has continued importance to the design of nuclear reactors and space exploration even today. He developed mathematical models for gamma radiation and invented radiation shields to protect against gamma radiation. Ernest designed optics for microscopes and eyeglasses. He also figured out the ideal shape of fins to expel heat from engines for cars, rockets, and more. All this work resulted in over a hundred papers in various fields, many of which are still relevant today!

BUILDING BUILDINGS

Have you ever wondered what the outside of a three-dimensional shape would look like if you "peeled it off" and laid it flat? J. Ernest Wilkins Jr. had to think about that when designing fins to expel heat from car and rocket engines. Let's do what he did!

THE MATH IN THE FUN

A **net** is what the outside of a three-dimensional shape would look like if it were opened up and drawn on a flat piece of paper.

For example, the net of a six-sided die is shownto the right.

In this project, we will make nets of some classic shapes, then fold the nets into three-dimensional shapes.

NOTE: Save these shapes for the Alien City activity, and feel free to color them so they look like alien buildings.

The net of a six-sided die.

Fig. 1. Net of a cube.

Fig. 2. Cut out the cube net.

Fig. 3. Fold along the lines.

MATERIALS

- Net templates from the back of the book (they can also be downloaded from www.mathlabforkids.com and https://quarto.com/files/MathForKids)
- Pencil
- Ruler or straightedge
- Paper (stock paper works best, although any paper will do)
- Colored pencils, crayons, or markers (optional)
- Scissors or craft knife
- Cutting mat if using a craft knife
- Tape

DIRECTIONS

MAKE THE NET OF A CUBE

1 With a pencil and ruler, draw a net like the one shown in "The Math in the Fun" box on page 18. A net with squares that are 2 by 2 inches (5.1 by 5.1 cm) will fit well on a standard 8.5-by-11-inch (21.6 by 28 cm) piece of paper. You can change the size of your squares to fit larger or smaller paper. Optional: If you use white paper for your net, feel free to color it creatively. *Fig. 1.*

2 With scissors, or a craft knife and cutting mat, cut the net along the outer edges. *Fig. 2.*

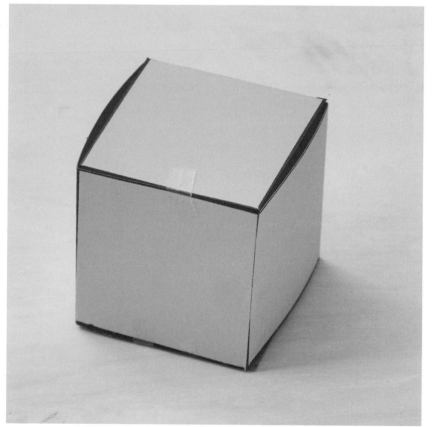
Fig. 4. Tape the sides.

3 Fold along the lines. If you are using a craft knife, it helps to lightly score along the lines before folding. *Fig. 3.*

4 Tape each side together. *Fig. 4.*

5 Admire your cube!

project continues ▶

MAKE THE NET OF A REGULAR TETRAHEDRON

An **equilateral triangle** is a triangle where all sides are the same length. A **regular tetrahedron** is a four-sided three-dimensional shape where all faces are the same-size equilateral triangle.

1 Copy the Tetrahedron Net template from the back of the book. It can also be downloaded from www.mathlabforkids.com and https://quarto.com/files/MathForKids.
Optional: If you used white paper for your net, color it creatively.

2 Cut along the edges of the outer equilateral triangle. *Fig. 5.*

3 Fold along the lines. If you are using a craft knife, it helps to lightly score along the lines before folding. *Fig. 6.*

4 Tape each side together. *Fig. 7.*

5 Admire your tetrahedron!

Fig. 5. Cut out the Tetrahedron Net.

Fig. 6. Fold along the lines.

Fig. 7. Tape the sides.

MAKE THE NET OF A SQUARE PYRAMID

Pyramids are named by the shape of their base. For example, a tetrahedron can also be called a **triangular pyramid**.

1 Copy the Square Pyramid Net template from the back of the book. It can also be downloaded from www.mathlabforkids.com and https://quarto.com/files/MathForKids. Optional: If you use white paper for your net, color it creatively.

2 Cut along the outer edges of the net. *Fig. 8.*

3 Fold along the edges of the square. If you are using a craft knife, it helps to lightly score along the lines before folding.

4 Tape each side together. *Fig. 9.*

5 Admire your square pyramid!

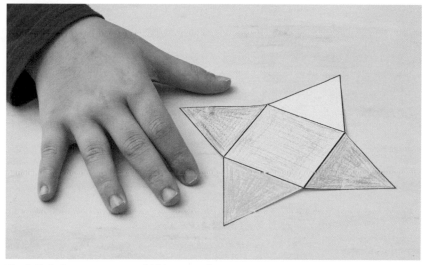

Fig. 8. Net of a square pyramid (decorated).

Fig. 9. Assembled square pyramid.

BONUS LEVEL

Can you make a net for the following?

- Octahedron
- Rectangular prism
- Triangular prism
- Or other shapes?
- What about a cone?

If you're stumped, you can find nets for an octahedron, rectangular prism, and triangular prism at www.mathlabforkids.com.

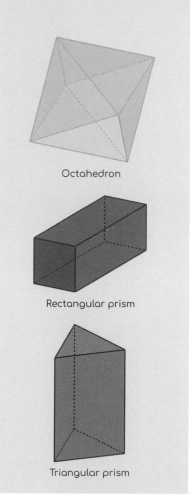

Octahedron

Rectangular prism

Triangular prism

GEOMETRY

Fan Chung

Born: October 9, 1949

YOUNG GENIUS

Fan Chung was born in Taiwan, the daughter of a brilliant engineer and a popular teacher. Her parents recognized Fan's intelligence when she was young and encouraged her academic pursuits. At National Taiwan University, Fan had several female peers who all encouraged and supported one another. Fan and her friend, Alice Chang, went on to have such impressive mathematical careers that a movie called *Girls Who Fell in Love with Math* was made about them.

IMMIGRATION TO THE UNITED STATES

Fan moved to the United States to go to graduate school at the University of Pennsylvania. Because she had the highest score on the qualifying exam, Herbert Wilf, the professor who would later become Fan's PhD adviser, asked if she would like to work on some problems with him. In one week, Fan came up with a major improvement to previous work in the field. This would end up being a large part of the work needed to get her PhD.

PARTNERSHIP WITH RON GRAHAM

Bell Labs was the largest and most prestigious non-university research institute in the world when Fan joined. While there, she met Ron Graham (whom you can also read about in this book). Thus began a thirty-seven-year mathematical and life partnership that was admired and envied by many. Together, Fan and Ron wrote more than a hundred significant papers and an influential book about one of their closest mathematician friends, titled *Erdős on Graphs: His Legacy of Unsolved Problems*.

THEORY BUILDER

Fan started her career solving interesting problems in graph theory and combinatorics, the math of combinations. Graph theory was invented in the eighteenth century but has become more important recently because it is the math

that describes the Internet and related areas. Over time, Fan became more of a theory builder. For example, she moved the field of spectral graph theory in a new direction by taking a geometric approach, which was a new way to look at it.

RETURN TO UNIVERSITY

In 1995, Fan became the first female tenured professor of mathematics at the University of Pennsylvania. In 1998, she moved to the University of California at San Diego, where she stayed for the rest of her career. Fan's book, *Spectral Graph Theory*, was published in 1997 and is still the main textbook on the subject in math graduate schools throughout the world. As of 2021, Fan had published more than two hundred papers and three influential books.

AWARDS AND HONORS

Dr. Fan Chung is a member of many societies but is most proud of being a fellow of the American Academy of Arts and Sciences, the American Association for the Advancement of Science, and the Academia Sinica. She was awarded the Allendoerfer Award of the Mathematical Association of America for writing excellence. Fan gave the 2009 American Mathematical Society Noether Lecture, a distinguished lecture series that honors women "who have made fundamental and sustained contributions to [math]." She also received the Euler Medal in 2017. The Euler Medal recognizes individuals with distinguished career contributions in combinatorics.

ART

As if she weren't talented enough, Fan is an accomplished watercolor painter. She paints landscapes and people, her subjects ranging from her grandchildren to famous mathematicians. Fan also plays the Chinese harp, known as a guzheng.

CORNERS AND EDGES AND FACES! OH MY!

One of Fan Chung's favorite areas of math is called graph theory. Learn some basic graph theory definitions and discover an amazing relationship between the edges, faces, and corners of three-dimensional shapes!

MATERIALS

- Pencil
- Paper
- 5 to 10 different solid shapes (see below for specifics)

We need to learn some math terms to do this project.

- A three-dimensional shape is **convex** if for every two points on the shape, you can draw a line between them that is completely contained within the shape. So for example, a three-dimensional star is *not* convex because the line between two corners is outside the shape. And any shape with a hole inside it is not convex.

- Mathematicians call corners of three-dimensional shapes **vertices**. (One corner is called a **vertex**.)

- The line between two vertices is called an **edge**.

- The side of a three-dimensional shape is called a **face**.

In the diagram of a cube in Figure 1, we have marked vertices in blue, edges in red, and faces in yellow. *Fig. 1.*

DIRECTIONS

1 Find five or more convex three-dimensional shapes with flat faces. You can use the nets you assembled in the Building Buildings activity; blocks with flat faces shaped like pyramids or prisms; dice in the shape of a tetrahedron, an icosahedron, or a dodecahedron; or whatever else you can find. *Fig. 2.*

2 We are going to count the number of edges, vertices, and faces of each shape. To track this information, it will be helpful to make a table like the one below on your piece of paper. *Fig. 3.*

Fig. 2. Convex solids: The only requirement is that the shapes are convex and have flat, not round, faces.

SHAPE	# OF VERTICES	# OF FACES	# OF EDGES

Fig. 3.

SHAPE	# OF VERTICES	# OF FACES	# OF EDGES
Cube	8	6	12
Square pyramid	5	5	8

Fig. 4.

Fig. 1.

Fig. 5.

3 Fill out the table for each of your shapes. We will help you with the first couple of rows. In the diagram of a square pyramid in Figure 5, we have marked the vertices, edges, and faces in the same colors as in the cube diagram in Figure 1. *Fig. 4* and *Fig. 5*.

4 Before you go on to the next step, do you notice anything? The mathematician who invented graph theory, Leonhard Euler, noticed a relationship between the number of vertices, number of faces, and number of edges for all convex three-dimensional solids. Can you figure it out?

5 Euler claimed that the (number of vertices) + (number of faces) - (number of edges) = 2 for all convex three-dimensional solids. Do you think he was right?

BONUS LEVEL

The (number of vertices) + (number of faces) - (number of edges) has a special name. It's called the **Euler characteristic** and it can be used to classify three-dimensional shapes.

1 Try finding some non-convex shapes and putting their entries into our table above. Was the Euler characteristic still 2?

2 Does a donut have an Euler characteristic? If yes, what is it and why?

THE MATH IN THE FUN

A **sphere** (the word mathematicians use for a ball) also has 2 for its Euler characteristic. To see why, imagine putting two points on opposite sides of the surface of a sphere (or really anywhere on the sphere's surface, but it's easiest to think about if they're on opposite sides) and connecting both points with two edges. (See diagram.) It's then easy to see that the Euler characteristic is 2 + 2 - 2 = 2. Now remove one of the edges. Then the sphere has a single face, one edge, and two points and the EC = 2 + 1 - 1, which is still 2. Now move the two points together so they merge into a single point. The edge will disappear and the EC will be 1 + 1 - 0 = 2.

The Euler characteristic is used to classify three-dimensional shapes. We just learned that the Euler characteristic of all convex three-dimensional solids is 2. If you could blow up any convex three-dimensional shape like a balloon, the shape would become a sphere. So it's to be expected that all convex three-dimensional shapes have the same Euler characteristic. This area of math is called **topology**. Topologists consider a cube and sphere (and any other shape with Euler characteristic 2) to basically be the same shape.

Nonconvex solids can have different Euler characteristics. For example, a topologist would say that a mug that has a handle is basically the same shape as a donut. Both a mug (with a handle) and a **torus** (the shape of a donut or bagel) have Euler characteristic 0.

Did you notice how we started out in graph theory and ended up in topology? The lines between various areas of math aren't so clear. There are lots of overlaps like these!

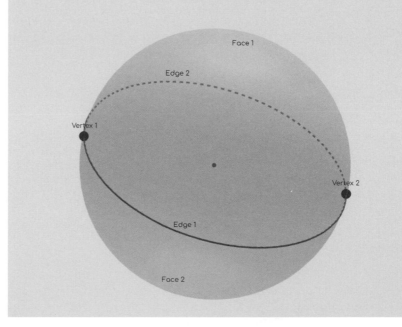

John Conway

December 26, 1937 – April 11, 2020

THE GOOFBALL

John Conway was an unpopular kid, so he decided to reinvent himself when he went to King's College, Cambridge University, in England. He became funny and outgoing, told great stories, and learned to laugh at himself. He succeeded in his goal so effectively that when it came time to apply for a job, the head of the math department at King's College wrote the letter of application for John. John was such a popular teacher that some students formed the John Conway Appreciation Society. A student described one memorable class where John completed a difficult proof while balancing a broom by its handle on his chin and juggling.

LOVE OF GAMES

While at King's College, John explored many different areas of math and discovered his love of games. He loved using math to determine the best strategy for games, or even to invent his own.

EARLY CAREER

For a while after John got his PhD, he felt lost, unsure of what to do next. He played a lot of games and worried he wasn't doing much math. Then someone told him about a twenty-four-dimensional structure called the Leech lattice. He decided he would work hard to learn something new about it. He set aside several days per week for a few months to do his research. But the very first evening, he made a major discovery that is now called the Conway Group. John made a number of discoveries and advanced many different areas of math and physics, including in group theory and knots. However, he is most well known for the Game of Life.

GAME OF LIFE

The Game of Life was one of the first-ever video games, though John described it as a "no-player never-ending" game. This Game of Life, nothing like the board game by the same name, has three rules: one for creating life, one for losing life, and one for survival. The idea of the game is to show how real animals live, die, and evolve. John showed the Game of Life to Martin Gardner (who is profiled on page 105), a mathematical journalist who wrote a recreational mathematics column for *Scientific American*. After Gardner wrote about the Game of Life, it became extremely popular and made John famous, even outside mathematics. The Game of Life has so much potential for discoveries that tons of mathematicians and programmers studied it and continue to do so even today.

OTHER ACCOMPLISHMENTS

In 1985, Dr. John Conway and several coauthors published the *ATLAS of Finite Groups*, considered by many to be the most important group theory book ever written. John wrote or co-wrote several other books too. His best seller was *Winning Ways for Your Mathematical Plays*, which is all about the math of various games. John was most proud of his discovery of **surreal numbers**, which resulted from his study of the game of Go. He was also proud of his work on the free will theorem and its influence on physics. John was a fellow of the American Academy of Arts and Sciences and the Royal Society, and received numerous awards, including being the first winner of the London Pólya Prize.

DOTS AND BOXES

John Conway loved applying math to games to help him win. See if you can do the same with the game Dots and Boxes, which you can play with a friend, sibling, or parent.

MATERIALS

- Dots and Boxes Board
- 2 different colored writing utensils
- 2 players

DIRECTIONS

1 Make a 5 × 5 grid yourself or download and print one from www.mathlabforkids.com. Feel free to play on the boards on page 29. *Fig. 1.*

RULES OF THE GAME

1 Each player picks a different color crayon, pencil, or pen.

2 Players take turns drawing a line between two dots that are next to each other. You can draw a line vertically or horizontally, but you cannot draw a diagonal line. *Fig. 2.*

3 If drawing a line lets you complete a box, color in that box with your color and take an extra turn. *Fig. 3.*

4 Once there are lines between every pair of dots, the game ends.

5 Each player counts the number of boxes of their color. The player with the most boxes of their color wins! *Fig. 4.*

Fig. 4. Completed game. Green wins!

BONUS LEVEL

Once you have played Dots and Boxes a few times, you can make your own game boards of any size. Try playing on a 6 × 6 or larger grid. It doesn't even have to be a square grid! It's a great game to play while waiting at a restaurant or doctor's office! If you don't have two different colored pencils, simply write each player's first initial inside their boxes.

THE MATH IN THE FUN

Dots and Boxes is a classic mathematical strategy game, first published in the nineteenth century by French mathematician Édouard Lucas. We can apply aspects of game theory to it to determine what our best moves are and even see what will happen turns ahead of time. For example, it is possible for a Dots and Boxes player to set up a "never-ending turn," where they create one box that leads them to another and another and so on. The setup for these chains begins far ahead of the never-ending turn. We can use mathematics to determine which player will get the never-ending stream of boxes and ultimately win the game.

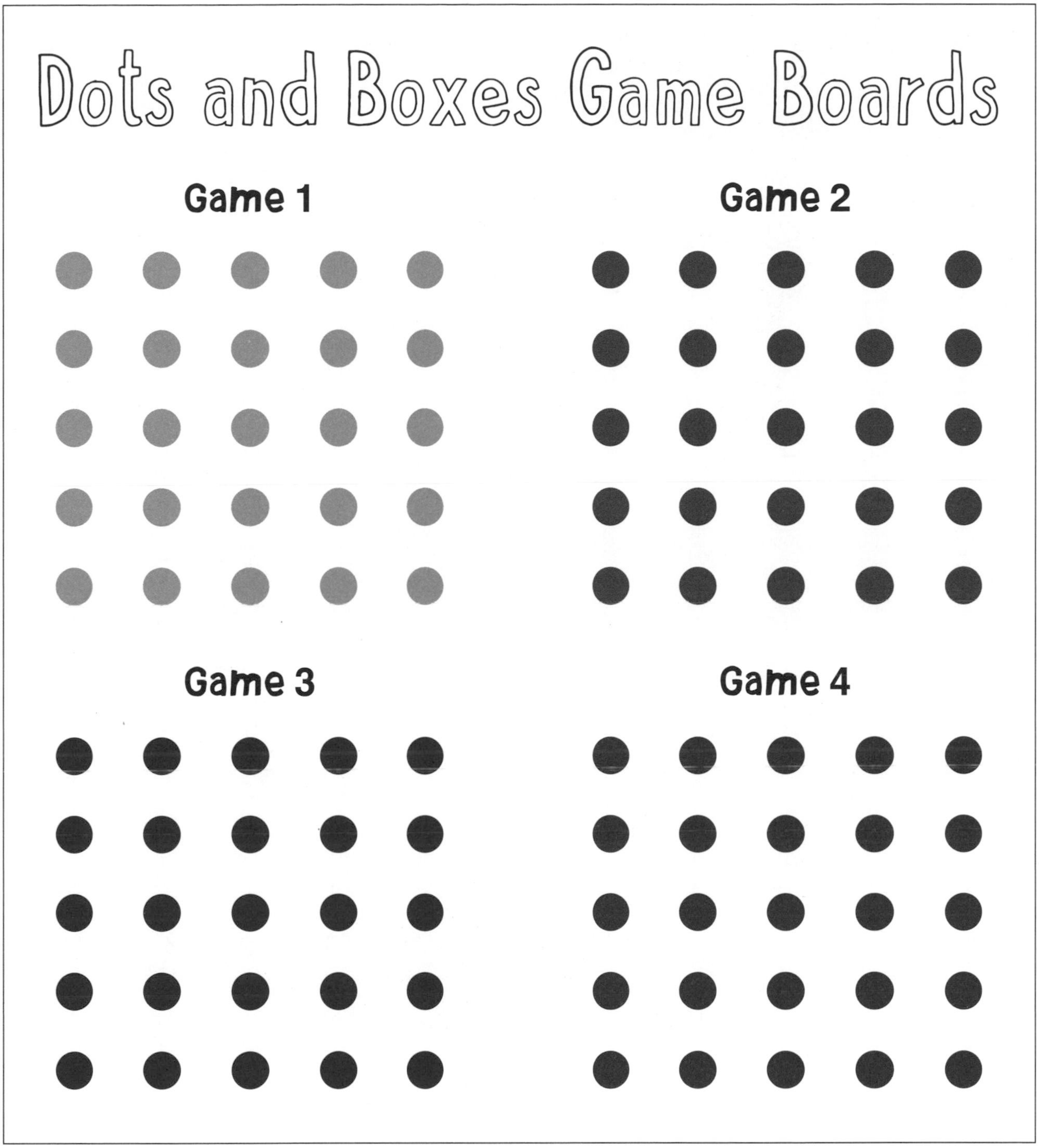

Dots and Boxes Game Boards

Game 1

Game 2

Game 3

Game 4

Fig. 1. Example game boards.

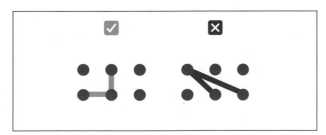

Fig. 2. Legal and illegal moves.

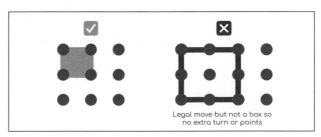

Legal move but not a box so no extra turn or points

Fig. 3. Claiming a box.

Federico Ardila

Born: April 5, 1977

MATH AND MUSIC

Federico Ardila is a mathematician and a DJ. That's not as surprising a combination as you might think. To Federico, music is one of the most powerful tools in the world for connecting people. He plays the marimba de chonta, a melodic percussion instrument made from trees from Colombian rainforests. He believes that both math and music can speak to all people, regardless of any differences. Federico uses music to "create an atmosphere where people can build bridges and connect." He cofounded the Oakland DJ collective La Pelenga to bring people together by introducing them to music from different cultures.

COLOMBIAN CHILDHOOD

As children growing up in Colombia, Federico's sister and cousin were the math whizzes in the family, not Federico. He didn't enjoy school, or even math classes, but he still placed first in the national math competition in fourth grade! In high school, he won a bronze medal in the International Math Olympiad in 1993 and a silver medal in 1994. Federico enjoyed the math competition scene, but his sister and cousin felt out of place because they thought that the math community was more welcoming of males. Hoping other girls won't feel excluded from math, Federico is working hard to make math a friendly and accepting community for all.

APPLYING TO MIT

One story Federico tells often is about how he ended up at MIT, one of the United States' best technical universities. He applied after a friend told him that MIT was an excellent place to study math and had awesome financial aid. Federico now says he would never have applied if he had known how selective MIT is because he didn't get good grades in high school. He hopes this story encourages students to reach for seemingly impossible things, as they just might come true.

MAKING CONNECTIONS

Federico's mathematical work forges connections between combinatorics (the math of combinations) and other diverse areas of math, including geometry, algebra, topology, and applied math. He spent five years working with another mathematician on unifying the geometric and algebraic sides of combinatorics. One night someone stole the backpack containing all their work. They were able to reconstruct it, but it took several years. Federico's work to make connections extends to his teaching, where one of his main goals is to make math a place in which his sister, cousin, and everyone else feels like they belong.

ARDILA'S AXIOMS

Dr. Federico Ardila received a National Science Foundation (NSF) CAREER grant that helped his inclusion goals. He created four axioms to promote diversity in mathematics. An **axiom** is a math statement that is assumed to be true and from which other math ideas follow. Ardila's axioms are ideas he believes are true, but that the math community doesn't necessarily treat as fact. For example, his first axiom is that mathematical potential is equally present in different groups, such as different races and economic classes. Unfortunately, the math community doesn't reflect this ideal, so Federico works really hard to encourage minority students to pursue math. His other axioms are that everyone can have fun with math, that math is powerful and can be used to help people in all kinds of situations, and that every student should be treated well. Federico's outreach work includes over two hundred hours of free math lecture videos.

PIGEONS LOVE HOLES

There are many really cool and easy-to-understand ideas in math. One of these, from the area of math called combinatorics—which happens to be one of Federico Ardila's specialties—is called the pigeonhole principle. In this activity we're going to learn all about it and even play a game.

MATERIALS

- 6 marbles or other small objects
- 6 small cups or bowls
- 2 six-sided dice
- 2 players

What is the **pigeonhole principle**? Let's explore to find out.

- Marbles represent pigeons and cups/bowls represent holes.

- Every pigeon *must* go into a hole, even if there's already another pigeon in the hole.

DIRECTIONS

1 Take six pigeons and five of your holes. *Fig. 1.*

2 Place pigeons into the holes according to the rules, with each pigeon being in a hole.

3 Can you make it so that each pigeon has its own hole while still following the rules?

Fig. 1. Six marbles (pigeons), five cups (holes).

The closest you can get is to put one pigeon in four of the holes and two in the fifth. This is the pigeonhole principle: If every pigeon must go into a hole, and there are more pigeons than holes, some pigeons will have to share their holes. *Fig. 2.*

Fig. 2. Two pigeons must share a hole!

Fig. 3. Player 1 rolls a 5.

Fig. 4. Player 2 rolls a 3.

Fig. 5. Player 1 places pigeons in holes.

RULES OF THE GAME

1 Player 1 rolls their die and places that many pigeons in front of them. *Fig. 3.*

2 Player 2 rolls their die and places that many holes in front of Player 1. *Fig. 4.*

3 Player 1 tries to place the pigeons in the holes according to the pigeonhole principle. If they succeed, they get a point. *Fig. 5.*

4 Repeat steps 1 to 3, this time with Player 2 rolling for pigeons, Player 1 rolling for holes, and Player 2 placing the pigeons in the holes.

5 Take turns back and forth until someone has five points. The first player to have five points wins!

BONUS LEVEL

- Create your own game using the pigeonhole principle.

- Use the pigeonhole principle to solve this riddle: If in a class of 32 people, every single one has a birthday in August, at least how many people share a birthday?

THE MATH IN THE FUN

The pigeonhole principle shows up all the time in real life, even at times you wouldn't expect. For example, because there are only twenty-six letters in the English alphabet, if you write twenty-seven or more letters, at least two of them have to be the same! If you're playing a game where you're rolling one six-sided die, you'll get a repeated roll at least every seven rolls. And maybe at school you have a group of five friends. If there are four classes, at least two of the friends will be in the same class! We can also combine the pigeonhole principle with probability. For example, in our scenario with five friends, what are the odds that three of them are together in class? Or two, two, and one? For even more math fun, try to figure out which setup is most likely.

$1^4 + 2^4 + 3^4 + \dots + n^4 = \frac{n^5}{5} + \frac{n^4}{2} + \frac{n^3}{3} - \frac{n}{30}$
$1^k + 2^k + 3^k + \dots + n^k = \frac{n^{k+1}}{k+1} + \frac{n^k}{2} + ???$
$\frac{1}{\pi} = \frac{2\sqrt{2}}{99^2} \sum_{k=0}^{\infty} \frac{(4k)!}{k!^4} \frac{26390k + 1103}{396^{4k}}$
$1729 = 1^3 + 12^3 = 9^3 + 10^3$
$\frac{1}{\pi} = \sum_{k=0}^{\infty} s(k) \frac{Ak+B}{C^k}$
$\sqrt{1 + 2\sqrt{1 + 3\sqrt{1 + \dots}}}$
$1 + 2 + 3 + \dots + n = \frac{n^2}{2} + \frac{n}{2}$
$1^2 + 2^2 + 3^2 + \dots + n^2 = \frac{n^3}{3} + \frac{n^2}{2} + \frac{n}{6}$
$1^3 + 2^3 + 3^3 + \dots + n^3 = \frac{n^4}{4} + \frac{n^3}{2} + \frac{n^2}{4}$
$1^4 + 2^4 + 3^4 + \dots + n^4 = \frac{n^5}{5} + \frac{n^4}{2} + \frac{n^3}{3} - \frac{n}{30}$
$1^k + 2^k + 3^k + \dots + n^k = \frac{n^{k+1}}{k+1} + \frac{n^k}{2} + ???$
$\binom{m+3}{m} B_m = \frac{m+3}{3} - \sum_{j=1}^{m/6} \binom{m+3}{m-6j} B_{m-6j}$, if $m \equiv 0 \pmod 6$;
$\frac{m+3}{3} - \sum_{j=1}^{(m-2)/6} \binom{m+3}{m-6j} B_{m-6j}$, if $m \equiv 2 \pmod 6$;
$-\frac{m+3}{6} - \sum_{j=1}^{(m-4)/6} \binom{m+3}{m-6j} B_{m-6j}$, if $m \equiv 4 \pmod 6$.
1729
1729

Srinivasa Ramanujan

December 22, 1887 – April 26, 1920

CHILD GENIUS

Part of the legend of Srinivasa Ramanujan is his fascinating mathematical partnership with G. H. Hardy. The two accomplished amazing things together. While Hardy was an extremely impressive English mathematician, he famously said that his greatest contribution to mathematics was discovering Srinivasa. Prior to their friendship, Srinivasa grew up as a poor child in India. His family was often sick. His three siblings all sadly passed away when they were very young. Srinivasa was often sick too, which luckily did not prevent him from being a very good student. He got the best scores in his whole district on all his exams when he was only ten years old! Only a year later, he was learning college-level math faster than most college students.

GETTING DEEPER INTO MATH

When Srinivasa was sixteen years old, he found a book that would change his life: *A Synopsis of Elementary Results in Pure and Applied Mathematics*. The book contained five thousand mathematical theorems, most with no proof. He became so obsessed with proving some of the theorems that he ignored many of his other classes, ultimately failing college. Nonetheless, he proved amazing mathematical results and published his first paper (on Bernoulli numbers) in the *Journal of the Indian Mathematical Society*.

MOVE TO ENGLAND

Srinivasa struggled to find a job that would allow him to focus wholly on math and make a decent wage. He decided to try to get in touch with some mathematicians in England. Most of the mathematicians to whom he sent letters thought he was a fraud. G. H. Hardy initially thought so too after receiving Srinivasa's long letter that included a ton of theorems. But fortunately, one of them caught his eye! Hardy was impressed by how much Srinivasa was able to accomplish while being completely self-taught. He could only imagine what Srinivasa could accomplish with more training, and the two quickly began sending letters back and forth. Hardy helped Srinivasa get a mathematical research job in India, then later arranged for Srinivasa to come to England. The two worked together in Cambridge for five years.

HEALTH ISSUES

Srinivasa was frequently sick. When he was around two years old, he caught smallpox, which he luckily survived. Later, he became sick again, this time requiring surgery. His family was very poor, but fortunately a doctor volunteered to help for free. When Srinivasa became sick again that same year, he was so afraid he would die that he gave his math notebooks to math professor Singaravelu Mudaliar, in case he didn't survive. Luckily, Srinivasa lived and was able to take his books back after recovering. However, he became sick once more when he moved to England. His religion's strict dietary requirements combined with food being rationed in England due to World War I worsened his condition. In 1919, Srinivasa went back to India, hoping that would help him recover. While it did help at first, he became sick again the next year and sadly passed away. Doctors have since studied his medical history and believe he suffered from undiagnosed amoebiasis, a parasitic disease that could have been cured had they known what it was.

MANCALA

Srinivasa Ramanujan studied number theory extensively. Number theory can help you win Mancala, a classic game where you try to collect as many marbles into your side of the board as you can. We're going to learn how to play Mancala on a handmade game board!

MATERIALS

- An empty egg carton that formerly held 12 eggs
- Scissors
- Tape
- 2 bowls
- 48 small objects (dried beans, coins, or marbles are great options)
- 2 players

Fig. 11. Each player takes a turn until one side is out of seeds.

DIRECTIONS

1 First, we need to create our game board. We only need the bottom half of the egg carton, so cut the top off using scissors. *Fig. 1.*

2 Next, tape a bowl to each short end of the egg carton. *Fig. 2.*

3 Finally, set up the game by placing four counters in each pit of the egg carton. Now you're ready to play! *Fig. 3.*

Fig. 1. Cut the top of an egg carton.

Fig. 2. Completed game board.

Fig. 3. Fully set-up game.

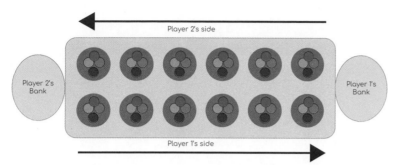

Fig. 4.

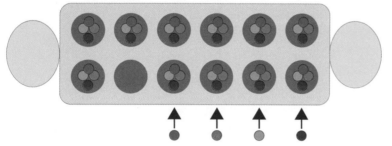

Fig. 5. Picking a pit.

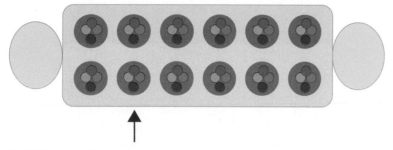

Fig. 6. Placing the seeds.

Fig. 7. Placed seeds.

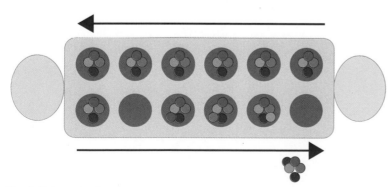

Fig. 8. Pick up the final pit.

RULES OF THE GAME

1 Players should sit opposite each other, each in front of one of the bowls. The bowl closest to each player is their "bank." Banks help with scoring at the end of the game.

2 Counters, called "seeds," move around the board in a counterclockwise direction. The six pockets, or pits, to the left of each player are that player's "side." *Fig. 4.*

3 Player 1 picks one of the pits on their side and picks up all of the seeds from that pit. They then move counterclockwise toward their bank, dropping one seed in each pit they pass on the way to their bank. *Fig. 5* and *Fig. 6* and *Fig. 7.*

4 When Player 1 runs out of seeds, they pick up all of the seeds in the pit where they placed their last seed and repeat step 3. *Fig. 8.*

project continues ▶

5 When Player 1 passes their bank, they place one seed into their bank and then continue placing seeds on Player 2's side. *Fig. 9.*

6 When Player 1 passes Player 2's bank, they do not place a seed into Player 2's bank. Instead, they place seeds on their own side, moving toward their bank. *Fig. 10.*

7 Repeat steps 3 to 6 until the final seed is dropped into an empty pit or is dropped into the active player's bank.

8 If the last seed is dropped into the active player's bank, the active player takes another turn, picking up all the seeds in one of the pits on their side.

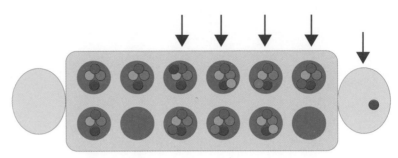

Fig. 9. Placing in personal bank.

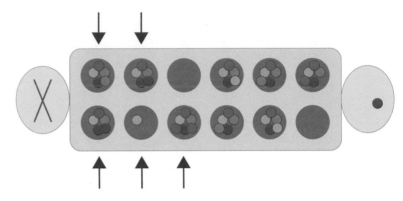

Fig. 10. Skip the opponent's bank.

THE MATH IN THE FUN

Mancala is one of the oldest recorded games we still play today. The game was invented in the third century or earlier and was probably played in ancient Sumeria and Egypt.

You can use math to help you form a winning strategy. Here are some good strategies according to the math. These strategies work especially well if you play with the capturing rule from the Bonus Level.

- Going first is a big advantage in Mancala. The first player can always get a free move on the first turn if they choose the right opening move. This move is considered the best opening. With the free move, you can set it up so your opponent cannot also take a free move.

- Make moves so that your pits have more than three seeds in them.

- On the flip side, try to make your opponent have fewer than three seeds in some of their pits. Picking up seeds from a pit that doesn't have very many seeds results in a shorter turn, and it's also easier for you to guess what your opponent will do.

The exception to the above stratagems is that you want to keep the pit to the left of your bank empty, because then you can move single seeds to get a free turn.

Fig. 11. The player with the most seeds in their bank wins!

9 If the last seed is dropped into an empty pit, the turn passes to Player 2.

10 Player 2 takes their turn in the same way that Player 1 did, but picks a pit on their own side and places seeds into their bank and not in Player 1's.

11 Continue taking turns until one side is out of seeds. All of the seeds on the nonempty side go into the bank of the player whose side they are on. *Fig. 11.*

12 Whoever has the most seeds in their bank at the end wins! *Fig. 12.*

BONUS LEVEL

Once you get good at the game, you can add one final rule—capturing! The way this works is if your last seed is dropped into an empty pit on your side, and the other player has seeds in the pit across from the one you landed in, you get to take all the seeds in both pits—the one you landed in and the one across—and place them in your bank!

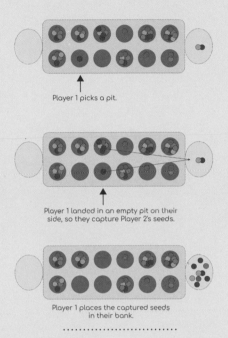

Player 1 picks a pit.

Player 1 landed in an empty pit on their side, so they capture Player 2's seeds.

Player 1 places the captured seeds in their bank.

Counting all of the seeds in each bank at the end of the game can take a while. Fortunately, all we need to know is who had more so we can tell who won. An easy way to figure out who has more is to have each player fill up their side with the seeds in their bank by placing four in each pit. This is great because it sets up for the next game *and* tells you who won. If both players filled their side, they had the same number of seeds and tied. Otherwise, one player will have extra seeds and the other player will be missing the same number of seeds. If that happens, the extra seeds should go on the other side so every pit in the game board has four seeds again.

If we double the number of extra seeds (which is the same as the number of missing seeds), we know how much the player won by! Why do we have to double the number of excess or missing seeds? See if you can figure it out.

Another interesting question: Since we are doubling the number of excess or missing seeds, the number a player won or lost by will always be even. Why?

If you're stumped, the answers to the above questions are in the Hints and Solutions section at the end of the book.

1 2 3 4 5 6 7 8 9 0

Muḥammad ibn Mūsā al-Khwārizmī

c. 780 – 850 CE

FATHER OF ALGEBRA

Muḥammad ibn Mūsā al-Khwārizmī is considered the father of modern algebra, a foundational area of math that most people learn in high school these days. In fact, "algebra" got its name from "al-Jabr" in the title of Muḥammad's book, *al-Kitāb al-Mukhtaṣar fī Ḥisāb al-Jabr wal-Muqābalah*, known in English as *The Compendious Book on Calculation by Completion and Balancing*. The book was translated into Latin in 1145 CE and used as the main math textbook in European universities for the next five hundred years!

DEVELOPMENT OF ALGEBRA

Muḥammad wrote *The Compendious Book on Calculation* to simplify and create a system for solving problems merchants commonly faced. The book laid out many of the main concepts of algebra. He was the first to develop the abstract concept of an equation and solving for general "unknowns" or "variables." He even used the Arabic word for "root," a term we still use. "Al-jabr," which means "restoration," refers to combining similar terms that appear on both sides of an equal sign so they appear on just one side. He also taught various methods to solve linear and quadratic equations.

ALGEBRA STANDS ALONE

Muḥammad was the first to treat algebra as a separate field of math. Previously, math was thought of in mostly geometric terms due to the huge Greek influence on math's early development. The important thing about algebra was it allowed math to do math on itself. Given that Muḥammad basically invented a whole new important area of math, it's no surprise that he is considered the greatest mathematician of his generation and one of the most influential mathematicians of all time!

ARITHMETIC ALGORITHMS

Muḥammad wrote another extremely influential book. The word "algorithm" comes from the version of Muḥammad's name that appears in the title of the Latin translation of the book, *Algoritmi de Numero Indorum*. He did not invent the Hindu-Arabic number system that uses the symbols 0, 1, …, 9, but he adopted them for his books. As his books were widely published and translated throughout Europe and the rest of the world, the number system spread too. The book also introduced the concepts of place value and using zero as a placeholder. The book also covered algorithms for addition, subtraction, multiplication, division, fractions, and decimals. Muḥammad's algorithms were adopted throughout Europe.

OTHER WORK

Around 820 CE, Muḥammad ibn Mūsā al-Khwārizmī became the head of the library and the chief astronomer of the House of Wisdom, a major intellectual center of his era. He created astronomical tables, calendars, and astrolabes. He made highly accurate sine and cosine tables that are important in astronomy and the first known table of tangents. He was part of a project to calculate the circumference of the Earth. Muḥammad also refined the theory of how to make sundials, which made them much easier to create and use going forward. After that, it became traditional to include a sundial at mosques to help identify the times to pray.

AWESOME ALGEBRA

You may have heard of algebra as being something scary, but it's actually really easy! In this activity, you're going to learn how to do algebra all by yourself the way that Muḥammad ibn Mūsā al-Khwārizmī did.

MATERIALS

- Stick or piece of string to act as a divider
- At least 24 counters or other small objects
- Bowl

NOTE: For this activity, left refers to the reader's left and right refers to the reader's right.

Fig. 4. Five counters in the bowl.

DIRECTIONS

1 In this activity, we will have two sides that we want to make equal. To make the sides clear, place a large stick or string in the middle of your workspace. We'll refer to the stick as the "divider." The workspace can be the floor or a table, as long as it is large enough to place counters on both sides. *Fig. 1.*

2 Place ten counters on the left side of the string and five on the right. Place the bowl on the right too. *Fig. 2.*

3 Our goal is to figure out how many counters we need to add to the right side to have the same number of counters on both sides of the divider. The bowl represents the answer.

4 Add counters one by one to the bowl until there are the same number of counters on each side. *Fig. 3.*

How many counters did you add? This is the answer. *Fig. 4.*

5 Congratulations, you just did algebra!

Fig. 1. Divided table.

Fig. 2. Problem setup.

Fig. 3. Equal counters on each side.

THE MATH IN THE FUN

The ideas we learned in this activity of adding or subtracting the same amount on both sides apply to other kinds of math as well! For example, we can multiply or divide each side by the same number and they will still be equal. This idea is super helpful for finding missing information, like how much more money you need to buy a pizza, and is important in all kinds of learning, especially in science! However, usually we don't use a bowl for algebra; instead, we write letters like the letter x to represent a number we don't know yet, but want to find out. Sometimes, if you get really good at algebra, you can even figure out multiple missing numbers at once!

project continues ▶

Pretty easy, right? Algebra is all about making things equal and using a **variable**. A variable is something that represents the answer before we know what the answer is. In this case, the bowl is our variable, and when it is filled, that is the answer!

Let's look at another problem.

1 Place five counters on each side of the divider. Leave the bowl out this time. *Fig. 5.*

2 Five is the same number as five, so if we have five on both sides, the sides are equal. Because our goal is for the sides to be equal, we are done, but let's explore what happens if we add or subtract counters.

3 Add three counters to the left and put the bowl on the right. *Fig. 6.*

4 Figure out how many counters need to be added to the bowl to make the sides equal again.

5 The answer is three! You probably knew this ahead of time. Why? *Fig. 7.*

Here's the answer: If five is the same as five, meaning they are equal, and then we add a number to one side, we need to add the same number to the other side to make them equal again. Similarly, if we take away two from the left side, then we need to take away two from the right to make the sides the same again. This is the most important idea behind algebra, that if you have two equal things and change them in the exact same way, then they will still be equal.

Fig. 5. Balanced sides of the divider.

Fig. 6. Three added to the right.

Fig. 7. Three must be added to the right.

Fig. 8. Problem setup.

Fig. 9. Subtract four from both sides.

Fig. 10. It works!

Let's put the two ideas we've explored together, but with a special rule: We want to find out how many counters need to go in the bowl without placing any in it.

1 Start with twelve counters on the left, four on the right, and the bowl on the right as well. *Fig. 8.*

2 We know the number of counters should be equal on both sides. The bowl represents how many counters the right needs to be equal to the left.

3 How can we keep both sides equal without adding to the bowl? Earlier, we were able to add or subtract from two equal things. The sides would be equal if we knew how many were in the bowl, so let's subtract.

4 Take away four counters from both sides. Now you should have eight counters on the left and just the bowl on the right. *Fig. 9.*

5 According to our rules, both sides of the divider should be equal, meaning the bowl equals eight counters.

6 Let's check our work. Set up the problem again, with twelve on the left and four and the bowl on the right. Since the bowl equaled eight, put eight counters into the bowl. Count up the counters on both sides. Twelve on both! *Fig. 10.*

Grace Hopper

December 9, 1906 – January 1, 1992

EARLY YEARS

When she was seven years old, Grace Hopper took apart seven alarm clocks to figure out how they worked. She attended Vassar College, graduating with honors in math and physics. Impressively, on top of being a full-time math professor at Vassar, Hopper found the time to earn a PhD, in math from Yale University.

JOINING THE NAVY

Grace was a math professor at Vassar for over a decade. When World War II broke out, she tried to enlist in the Navy but was rejected because, at age thirty-four, she was considered too old; her weight was fifteen pounds below the Navy's minimum; and most importantly, her job as a mathematician and math professor was considered too important to the war effort. Grace refused to give up and joined the U.S. Navy Reserves instead, although she had to get an exemption because of her weight. She was assigned to a very early computer project at Harvard University. Their computer, the Mark I, was 51 feet (15.5 m) long, 8 feet (2.4 m) high, 8 feet (2.4 m) wide, and could only do three additions per second.

FIRST COMPUTER BUG

Grace continued to work on the Harvard computing project even after World War II ended. One night, a computer malfunctioned. Eventually, someone figured out there was a moth inside the computer! Grace later explained, "From then on, when anything went wrong with a computer, we said it had bugs in it." She taped the moth to a logbook where you can still see it at the Smithsonian Museum. To this day, finding errors in a computer program is called "debugging."

ENGLISH-BASED PROGRAMMING LANGUAGE

Grace understood long before most people just how useful computers could be in the business world. Early programming required significant math and computer knowledge. She developed a programming language that looked closer to English to make programming easier and allow more people to work with computers. This was successful, but there was soon a problem because every type of computer had its own language. So then, Grace helped lead a group that standardized computer language for business. The result was Common Business Oriented Language (COBOL). Next, she worked on convincing the Navy to adopt COBOL.

COMPUTER AMBASSADOR

Dr. Grace Hopper was a great speaker and teacher. She was a tireless advocate for the simplification, standardization, and wider adoption of computers. She retired from the Navy twice, only to be recalled to active service each time as they needed her to lead important projects, such as standardizing the Navy's computer use. Grace was seventy-nine when she retired from the Navy for the third and final time.

AWARDS AND HONORS

Grace retired from the Navy with the high rank of rear admiral. She received almost fifty honorary university degrees, the Presidential Medal of Freedom, and many military medals, including the Legion of Merit, and she was buried with full honors in Arlington National Cemetery. She was the first woman to be the sole winner of the National Medal of Technology, the United States' highest technology award. Yale University even renamed one of its colleges after her. She was elected to the American Academy of Arts and Sciences, had multiple scholarships and awards established in her name, and inspired a yearly conference for women in computing. Grace also had a U.S. Navy boat and a planet named after her!

BINARY BRACELET

ASCII, which is short for American Standard Code for Information Interchange, is used to encode the letters of the alphabet into computer language, like Grace Hopper did. We're going to use ASCII to make a bracelet that contains a secret code!

MATERIALS

- Beads in three different colors
- Pencil or pen
- Paper
- Ruler
- Scissors
- Yarn, string, wire, or a pipe cleaner

Binary codes use only 0s and 1s, which are called **bits**. When coding for computers, we often want some way to indicate that a letter, word, or something else has ended and we're about to start a new one. We call the indicator a **delimiter**.

DIRECTIONS

PREPARE YOUR CODE

1 Choose one color bead to use for 1s, a second color to use for 0s, and a third color to use for delimiters. In our example, we chose black for 1s, white for 0s, and red for delimiters.

2 Decide what you want to encode in your bracelet. It could be your initials, your name, or another short word. Or if you want to encode something longer, you can make a binary necklace instead of a bracelet. In our example, we will encode the name "Zack."

NOTE: Beads that are 8mm in diameter are large enough that you will only have room for your initials if you are making a bracelet. You can encode a longer message in a necklace or if you use smaller beads.

3 Look up each letter in the "ASCII to Text Conversion Table" and write it down on your paper. We're encoding "Zack," so we write down: Z: 1011010, a: 1100001, c: 1100011, k: 1101011.

Fig. 4. Binary code for "Zack."

ASCII to Text Conversion Table			
ASCII	LETTER	ASCII	LETTER
1000001	A	1100001	a
1000010	B	1100010	b
1000011	C	1100011	c
1000100	D	1100100	d
1000101	E	1100101	e
1000110	F	1100110	f
1000111	G	1100111	g
1001000	H	1101000	h
1001001	I	1101001	i
1001010	J	1101010	j
1001011	K	1101011	k
1001100	L	1101100	l
1001101	M	1101101	m
1001110	N	1101110	n
1001111	O	1101111	o
1010000	P	1110000	p
1010001	Q	1110001	q
1010010	R	1110010	r
1010011	S	1110011	s
1010100	T	1110100	t
1010101	U	1110101	u
1010110	V	1110110	v
1010111	W	1110111	w
1011000	X	1111000	x
1011001	Y	1111001	y
1011010	Z	1111010	z

Fig. 1. Knot the string.

Fig. 2. Encode the first letter (example: "Z").

Fig. 3. Add a delimiter bead.

MAKE YOUR BRACELET

1 With a ruler and scissors, measure and cut a piece of string 3 inches (7.6 cm) longer than you want the final bracelet or necklace to be.

2 Tie a big knot at one end of your string. Make sure the knot is big enough that the beads won't slip off. You will probably want to tie a double or triple knot. *Fig. 1.*

3 Using the colors you chose for 1s and 0s, string them in order for your first letter. Our example shows "Z." *Fig. 2.*

4 Add a delimiter bead at the end of your first letter. *Fig. 3.*

5 Repeat steps 3 and 4 until you have spelled your entire coded message. Our example shows "Zack." *Fig. 4.*

6 Cut the string so it is a few inches longer than what is needed to fit around your wrist. If you're making a necklace, cut the string a few inches longer than you want the necklace to be.

7 Tie the bracelet closed but leave a little extra space so you can slip it on and off.

8 Cut off the extra string but not too close to the end so the knots don't come undone.

BONUS LEVEL

- We don't actually need to use delimiters. Why not?

- Look at the codes for a few matching uppercase and lowercase letters. What is the same? What is different?

- Can you read the message in this bracelet?

Secret message for you to decode.

If you're stumped, the answers to the above questions are in the Hints and Solutions section at the end of the book.

THE MATH IN THE FUN

ASCII is based on an even older code used by telegraphs, which were machines that transmitted messages long distances. ASCII was originally seven characters long, and that's what we used for this project. These days, most implementations use eight characters because with computers, everything comes in powers of two and eight is the smallest power of two in which a reasonable amount of information can be encoded. ASCII actually encodes much more than just the alphabet. It also contains numbers, other characters such as the % sign, and also codes that were used to control telegraph machines. Many of the last group are no longer used, but tab, return, and a few others still are.

Mary Everest Boole

March 11, 1832 – May 17, 1916

FALLING IN LOVE WITH MATH

When Mary Everest was very young, her family moved from England to France, where her math tutor, Monsieur Deplace, inspired her fascination with math. He was such a great teacher that Mary was devastated when she had to move back to England. Back home, Mary was disappointed to learn that because she was a woman, she was unable to attend university to continue studying math. She resolved to teach herself, learning calculus from her father's books and talking to many of her father's mathematician friends. Her uncle, George Everest, also encouraged Mary by introducing her to mathematician George Boole when she was eighteen. Mary and George developed a strong friendship over their shared love of math and wrote each other letters for several years.

A MATHEMATICAL FAMILY

When Mary was twenty-three, she married George Boole. She attended his lectures and helped him with his work. Sadly, he died nine years later when their youngest child was only six months old, leaving Mary to raise five daughters on her own. Mary's eldest daughter, Alicia Boole Stott, followed in her parents' footsteps and became a respected mathematician. Lucy Everest Boole, Mary's second child, became a chemist and broke through many barriers for women, including becoming the first female professor at the London School of Medicine and the first female fellow of the Royal Institute of Chemistry. Mary's youngest daughter, Ethel, made a name for herself as a novelist. Mary's uncle, George Everest, used math to figure out the height of the mountain that is now named after him.

CAREER

Shortly after her husband's death, Mary got a job as a librarian at Queens College, London, the first women's college in England. Mary wanted to teach math and science, but at the time, women were not allowed to teach or even earn degrees. As a librarian, however, she was able to tutor students who came to the library. Not only did she love teaching, but she was also good at it. Mary channeled her love of teaching into writing books, including the controversial *The Message of Psychic Science for Mothers and Nurses*. Her belief in the influence of the supernatural eventually caused her to lose her librarian job. After that, she took a job as a secretary for her father's friend, James Hinton. While working for James, Mary became interested in evolution and corresponded with Charles Darwin. Mary went on to write other books that were extremely well received.

MARY'S INFLUENCE ON TEACHING PERSISTS TODAY

Mary Everest Boole is best known for her innovative methods of teaching math and science to children. Her books *The Preparation of the Child for Science* and *Philosophy and Fun of Algebra* discussed how children learn. She advocated for hands-on teaching methods that allowed children to explore math through playful activities. Mary also encouraged critical thinking and urged careful use of repetition. These books were highly respected and influenced the development of many schools in England and the United States. Many of Mary's methods are still used in Montessori and other schools today.

STITCHING EVEREST

Mary Everest Boole invented curve stitching as a hands-on way for kids to learn math concepts. In this project, you'll learn to draw curves using straight lines and also how to stitch beautiful mathematical art, just like Mary Everest Boole!

DRAWING CURVES USING STRAIGHT LINES

MATERIALS

- Stitching Everest template (Use a blank piece of graph paper to make your own Stitching Everest template or you can download the template from www.mathlabforkids.com.)
- Ruler or straightedge
- Pen, marker, or pencil (multiple colors preferred)

DIRECTIONS

1 Download and print out a copy of the Stitching Everest template from www.mathlabfor-kids.com or make a copy of the Stitching Everest template. *Fig. 1.*

2 Using a ruler and a pencil, draw a straight line from the point labeled 1 in the upper left corner to the points labeled 1 on the top *and bottom* of the square. *Fig. 2.*

3 Repeat step 2 for points labeled 2 through 15. *Fig. 3.*

4 Repeat steps 2 and 3 starting with the point labeled 1 in the lower right corner of the square. (Use a different color if you like.) *Fig. 4.*

Fig. 12. Complete four-pointed star.

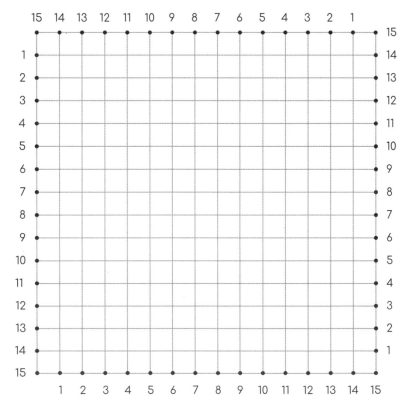

Fig. 1. Stitching Everest template.

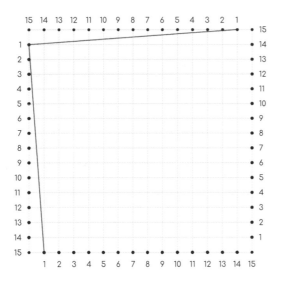

Fig. 2. Connect the 1s with straight lines.

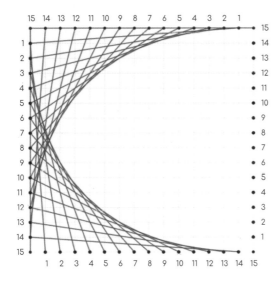

Fig. 3. Connect the 2s, 3s, ... , 15s with straight lines.

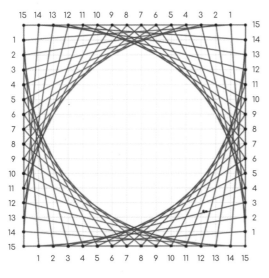

Fig. 4. Draw straight lines to make the remaining curves.

BONUS LEVEL

- Try the activity with five or twenty points on each side of the square. What is different?

- Try the same activity starting with a triangle or a plus sign instead of a square. (We got you started in the figures below.)

If you're stumped, there are examples of completed curves using the templates below in the Hints and Solutions section on page 116.

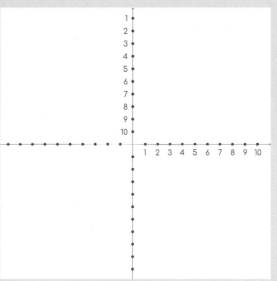

Plus sign template for curves.

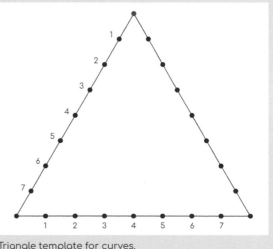

Triangle template for curves.

project continues ▶

CURVE STITCHING

When Mary Everest Boole devised this activity, called "curve stitching," she intended for kids to poke holes in something and pull string through the holes. Let's try it!

MATERIALS

- Ruler
- Pencil
- Cardstock
- Graph paper (optional)
- Tape
- Pushpin
- Corrugated cardboard
- Scissors
- Embroidery floss or yarn
- Large eye blunt "yarn" needle (large enough so your embroidery floss or yarn is easy to thread, and blunt enough you won't accidentally hurt yourself)

DIRECTIONS

1 Use a ruler and pencil to draw and label the plus sign image shown in the "Bonus Level" box on page 53 onto a piece of cardstock. You could use graph paper to make the plus sign, then tape it to the cardstock if you prefer. Alternatively, print a downloadable version of the image from www.mathlabforkids.com directly onto the cardstock.

2 Use a pushpin to carefully poke a hole at each mark on your cardstock. This is easier to do if you put your cardstock over something you can push pins into safely, like a piece of corrugated cardboard. *Fig. 5.*

3 Cut a piece of embroidery floss or yarn about the length of your arm and thread it onto your needle.

4 Starting from the back of your cardstock, push the needle through the hole you labeled number 1 at the top. As you pull the embroidery floss through the hole, stop when there are a couple of inches still sticking through and tape the end of the floss down on the BACK of the cardstock very securely. Tug on the floss a little to make sure it won't slip through. *Fig. 6.*

5 Your needle should be on the front side of your cardstock now. Push the needle through the other hole marked number 1 to make a long stitch. The yarn should connect the two dots, just like we did when drawing curves above. *Fig. 7.*

Fig. 5. Poke holes in the cardstock.

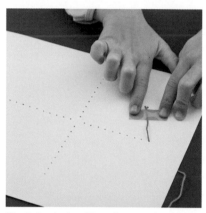
Fig. 6. Back view: Tape floss to the back of the cardstock.

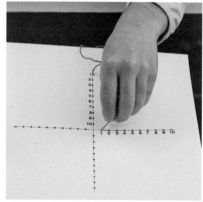
Fig. 7. Front view: Push the needle through the other hole 1.

6 Starting on the back of your cardstock again, push the needle through the hole right next to it, which should be hole number 2, making a short stitch. Then, from the front side, you can make another long stitch to connect the two number 2 holes. *Fig. 8* and *Fig. 9.*

7 Continue like this for the rest of the holes. You should have long stitches on the front side of your cardstock and short stitches on the back. If you run out of yarn before you're done, tape the end down on the *back* of your cardstock, cut another piece of floss, thread your needle, and keep going. When you've finished the curve, tape the end of the floss on the back of the cardstock and trim any long ends. *Fig. 10* and *Fig. 11.*

8 Stitch the other three curves in the same way to make a four-pointed star! You can number the other holes if that makes it easier for you to visualize what to connect. Experiment with different colors of embroidery floss. *Fig. 12* (page 52).

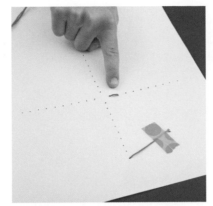

Fig. 8. Back view: the second stitch.

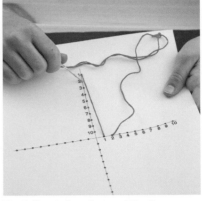

Fig. 9. Front view: Connect the 2s.

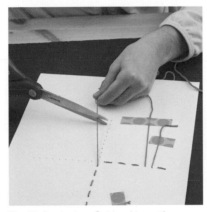

Fig. 10. Back view: Cut and tape the final stitch.

Fig. 11. Front view: the final stitch.

BONUS LEVEL

Can you use this method to make a three-pointed star or a five-pointed star?

THE MATH IN THE FUN

Numerical analysis is a branch of mathematics that studies how to use easy-to-compute methods to find approximate solutions to problems that are too difficult to solve directly. Numerical algorithms are usually done on a computer. By doing more calculations, you can refine your approximate solution.

In this project, we approximate a curve using only straight lines. The closer you draw the lines together (the more points you put on each side of the square), the better approximation you make. Imagine how close you could come to a curve if you used fifty points on a side, or a hundred! This is an example of how a numerical analysis algorithm allows you to get as close as you want to the true solution by changing the number of computations you do.

Ron Graham

October 31, 1935 – July 6, 2020

JUGGLING AND TRAMPOLINE

Ron Graham was a giant among mathematicians, both because he had a huge influence on many areas of modern math and because he was over 6 feet (1.8 m) tall. Ron started at the University of Chicago when he was fifteen. He did so well in the math portion of his scholarship qualifying exams that he didn't take any math classes while he was there. However, he did learn how to juggle and participated in many gymnastics contests, especially on the trampoline. He was the California state trampoline champion and supported himself through graduate school at the University of California, Berkeley by founding a professional trampoline troupe called the Bouncing Baers.

MATH OUTREACH

Ron was great at showing nonmathematicians how interesting and useful math can be. He is in the *Guinness Book of World Records* for Graham's number, the largest number ever used in a mathematical proof. Graham's number is so big that there is not enough space in the known universe to write it down! Ron was featured in *Ripley's Believe It or Not!* He also consulted and juggled on stage with Cirque du Soleil.

MATH AND MAGIC

Ron was quite interested in the mathematics of magic. He and Persi Diaconis (whom you can also read about in this book) wrote a book called *Magical Mathematics: The Mathematical Ideas That Animate Great Magic Tricks*. The book won the Euler Book Prize for "an outstanding book in mathematics that is likely to improve the public view of the field."

APOLLO MOON MISSION

Ron worked on scheduling problems and pioneered the area of worst-case analysis, a method for finding the worst possible outcome of a situation. NASA even sought his expertise on the Apollo moon mission. NASA was worried that the astronauts' schedules were flawed. Ron was able to reassure them that the schedules were within a few percentage points of the best possible outcome and certainly good enough.

PROLIFIC MATHEMATICIAN

In addition to the math mentioned earlier, Ron developed much of the math of juggling. He also studied the math of telephones and the Internet. He researched Ramsey theory, soap bubbles, Fibonacci numbers, and much more. Ron loved numbers so much that his license plate was "NUMBER." He wrote more than four hundred papers, including more than a hundred with his wife, fellow mathematician Fan Chung (profiled earlier in this book). Their mathematical and life partnership was admired and envied by many.

ALWAYS THE ENTERTAINER

Ron sometimes showed up to give talks with a mysterious satchel. After his talk, he would encourage people to meet him at a nearby field. He would open the mysterious satchel to reveal many boomerangs and then proceed to teach everyone present how to throw a boomerang.

CHARISMATIC LEADER

A charismatic leader, Dr. Ron Graham worked at Bell Labs, which was considered the most prominent research lab outside a university, for thirty-seven years, rising to the level of chief scientist. He was the first person to be president of both the American Mathematical Society and the Mathematical Association of America. He was also the president of the International Jugglers' Association. Ron was elected to the National Academy of Sciences and won the American Mathematical Society's Steele Prize for Lifetime Achievement.

FIBONACCI SPIRAL

Ron Graham loved playing with the famous Fibonacci sequence. In this activity, we'll make an artistic representation of the Fibonacci sequence.

MATERIALS

- 12-inch (5 cm) chenille stems or pipe cleaners
- 8mm beads in five or more colors

NOTE: Save the finished spiral for the Alien City activity (on page 112).

Fig. 9. The "opened" spiral.

THE MATH IN THE FUN

There is a famous sequence of numbers that appears frequently in nature and also in mathematical patterns. Many people call it the **Fibonacci sequence** because an Italian mathematician named Fibonacci wrote about it in the Middle Ages. However, mathematicians from other cultures studied it too, way before Fibonacci. Acharya Pingala, an Indian poet and mathematician, knew about the sequence in the third or second century BCE!

The sequence is constructed by adding the previous two numbers to get the next one. The first two numbers are 1. The third number is 2, which is 1 + 1. The fourth number is 3, which is 1 + 2. The fifth number is 5, which is 2 + 3. And so on. The first few numbers in the sequence are: 1, 1, 2, 3, 5, 8, 13, 21, 34, 55, 89, and 144. Fibonacci numbers appear so often in math that there is an entire journal to study them, *Fibonacci Quarterly*.

Some people say the Fibonacci sequence starts with 0 and 1 instead of 1 and 1. If you think about it, you'll realize that the sequence continues the same way whether the first number is 1 or 0.

Fig. 1. Make a knot.

Fig. 2. String the first bead.

Fig. 3. String second bead in a *new* color.

DIRECTIONS

1 Make a knot at one end of a chenille stem so your beads won't fall off. You can fold one end if you prefer, just make sure the beads won't come off. *Fig. 1.*

2 String one bead onto the chenille stem and push it all the way to the end until the knot prevents it from going further. Really test your knot to make sure the bead can't slip off. *Fig. 2.*

3 String a second bead *in a different color from the first bead* and push it all the way to the end so it's snug against the first bead. *Fig. 3.*

project continues ▶

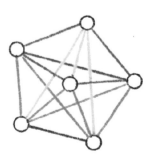

4 From now on, we'll be increasing the number of beads we string each time to follow the Fibonacci sequence. String two beads of a *new* color. *Fig. 4.*

5 String three beads of a *new* color. *Fig. 5.*

6 String five beads of a *new* color. *Fig. 6.*

7 At this point, you have used five different colors. If you have more colors, keep going with new colors as long as you can. At some point, you will have to start reusing colors. The most important thing is to not use the same color for two numbers in a row. We think it's prettiest if you use the same order for your colors, but feel free to be creative as long as you don't reuse the same color for two Fibonacci numbers in a row. String eight beads.

8 String thirteen beads.

9 At this point, you probably don't have much room left on your chenille stem. Take a new chenille stem and twist it together with the one that contains your beads. Make sure the stems are twisted together really well. When you string the next set of beads, have them cover where the stems are twisted together. *Fig. 7.*

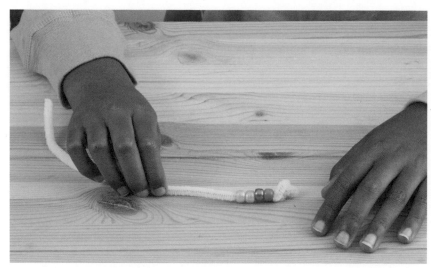

Fig. 4. String two more beads in *another* color.

Fig. 5. String three beads in a *new* color.

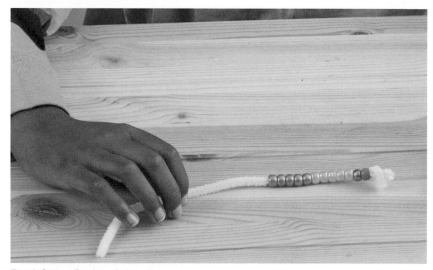

Fig. 6. String five beads in a *new* color.

10 Keep stringing ever increasing Fibonacci numbers until you get bored, adding more stems as in step 9 if needed. We ended up using three chenille stems and stopped after adding fifty-five beads of the same color.

11 Now we're going to turn our creation into a spiral. Lay your handiwork on a flat surface. Starting at the knotted end, slowly curl the whole object around itself, keeping it as flat and tightly wound as possible. *Fig. 8.*

12 Now let go. The spiral will "open up" beautifully. *Fig. 9.*

Fig. 7. Twist the chenille stems together tightly.

Fig. 8. Tightly curl the spiral around itself.

BONUS LEVEL

Consecutive (two in a row) Fibonacci numbers appear frequently in nature. You can find them in pine cones, ferns, pineapples, sunflowers, leaves on a branch, and many more places. For example, look at a pine cone from the top or bottom and count the number of spirals going from the center out to the sides (blue lines in this photo). Then count spirals going from the sides into the center (red lines in this photo). The number should be the next highest or lowest Fibonacci number!

Go on a hunt through nature looking for numbers from the Fibonacci sequence. You'll often find them in pairs.

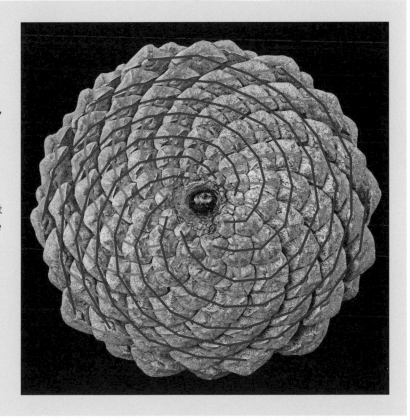

Jennifer McLoud-Mann

Born: June 21, 1975

PENTAGONAL TILING DISCOVERY

In 2015, Jennifer McLoud-Mann and her husband, mathematician Casey Mann, with the help of University of Washington Bothell student, David Von Derau, wrote a computer program that found the fifteenth type of pentagon that can "tile the plane." A shape can tile the plane if you can use many copies of it to cover a flat surface without gaps or overlaps. Many bathroom floors (without the grout) provide a good example of mathematical tiling. All three- and four-sided shapes can tile the plane. Mathematicians had previously classified all six-sided convex shapes that could tile the plane. But the question of convex pentagons (five-sided shapes) was still open. Jennifer was interested in this question because "the cool thing in mathematics is that sometimes you have a simply stated problem that doesn't have a simple solution." The fifteenth pentagon was the first new pentagon discovered to tile the plane in thirty years! Jennifer had begun to wonder whether they would ever succeed because it took them two years to find it. After hearing about the discovery, French mathematician Michael Rao created a computer-assisted proof that there can only be fifteen. So it turns out that Jennifer and her team found the last possible pentagon to tile the plane!

CAREER

Jennifer was the first college graduate in her family and received a PhD from the University of Arkansas, Fayetteville. She is currently a professor and the associate dean for the School of STEM at the University of Washington (UW) Bothell. Her main research areas are knot theory, combinatorics, tiling theory, and commutative algebra. She enjoys collaborating with other mathematicians and undergraduates. She is also interested in shaping how college students are taught mathematics. Jennifer loves to teach mathematics courses where curious students learn how to show why math works!

ENCOURAGING FUTURE MATHEMATICIANS

Dr. Jennifer McLoud-Mann is committed to encouraging students from underrepresented groups to pursue careers in mathematics because of her experiences as a first-generation Native American woman of the Cherokee Nation. For example, she organized Sonya Kovalevsky Day festivals several years in a row. During these festivals, high school women were invited to the University of Texas (UT) at Tyler for a day of mathematical activities and encouraged to pursue math-related careers. She has led Research Experience for Undergraduates (REU) sites at two universities to give students a taste of math research. The REUs have specifically selected minority, women, and first-generation college students to encourage them to go to math graduate school. Jennifer has also served as an adviser to the UT Tyler and UW Bothell Mathematics Societies, where she helps college students see what it's like to be a professional mathematician.

AWARDS

Jennifer's emphasis on good teaching has been recognized by her peers. She won the Mathematical Association of America's Henry L. Alder Award for Distinguished Teaching by a Beginning College or University Mathematics Faculty Member and the White Fellowship for Teaching at UT Tyler. She also received UW Bothell's Distinguished Research, Scholarship, and Create Activity Award.

SHAPE-SHIFTING

Jennifer McLoud-Mann works with tiling, and you can too! A shape can "tile the plane" if you can use many copies of it to cover a flat surface with no gaps and no overlaps. In this activity, you'll create a fun shape to tile a piece of paper!

MATERIALS

- Index card or other rectangle
- Pencil
- Scissors
- Tape
- Markers, crayons, or colored pencils
- Paper

Fig. 8. Fully tiled decorated sheet.

DIRECTIONS

1 We start with a rectangle. You can carefully measure one, or just use an index card for your rectangle.

2 With a pencil, make a design on one edge. It can be as complicated as you want but make sure it goes all the way from the top to the bottom. Cut it out with scissors. *Fig. 1.*

3 Tape the cut piece to the opposite side. *Fig. 2.*

4 Decide what your design looks like. In our example, it could be a dog or a turtle. With different decorations, the same shape can look quite different! Decorate your design. *Fig. 3* and *Fig. 4.*

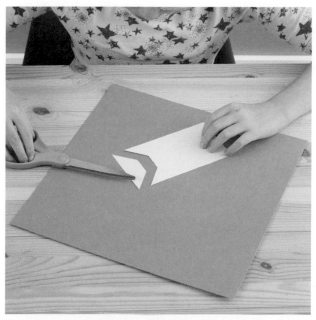
Fig. 1. Cut a design from one side.

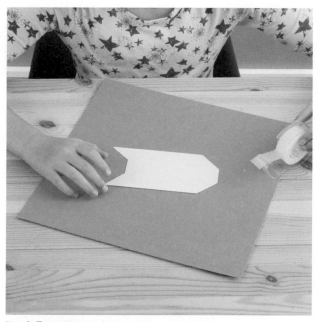
Fig. 2. Tape the cut design to the other side.

Fig. 3. Decorate your design.

Fig. 4. Decorate your design a different way.

project continues ▶

5 Carefully trace your shape on a piece of paper starting in the bottom left or right corner. Then slide the shape to the left or right so the cut edges line up and trace the shape again. This is called **translating** the shape. Keep going until you fill up the row. *Fig. 5.*

6 When you get to the second row, you can shift your shape over a little. Or you can start it all the way to the side like you did with the first row.

7 Keep going until you fill up the paper with copies of your shape. It's okay, and expected, that you'll have some partial pieces of your shape. *Fig. 6.*

8 Now decorate! You can decorate all the shapes the same way, decorate them all differently, or alternate decorations. In one of our examples, we switched between turtles and dogs, and decorated them all a little differently. In another example, we decorated using solid colors. *Fig. 7* and *Fig. 8.*

Fig. 5. Trace the shape, then slide it and trace again.

Fig. 6. Trace the shape over the whole paper.

Fig. 7. Fully tiled decorated sheet using solid colors.

BONUS LEVEL

In this project, we cut a piece from one side and taped it to the other. You can cut a piece from the top and tape it to the bottom (or vice versa) *in addition*. This will create an even more interesting shape that will still tile the plane such as the tessellations below (left). Try it! You can make tessellations starting from other shapes too. For example, the elephant tessellations below (right) did not start from a rectangle. Can you figure out what shape was their foundation?

Wood tessellations.

THE MATH IN THE FUN

This project explored how to tile the plane. The shape you made is called a **tile**, and a plane is a flat two-dimensional surface. Using multiple tiles to cover a plane is called a **tessellation** or a **tiling**. The famous artist M. C. Escher created a lot of well-known and beautiful mathematical art. When he was young, Escher traveled to Spain, where he visited a renowned Moorish building called the Alhambra. The Alhambra contains many intricate repeating designs that inspired Escher's lifelong interest in tessellations. Escher thought he was no good at math, but many mathematicians befriended him and appreciated his art. Escher became famous late in life after being featured in an article by Martin Gardner (whom you can also read about in this book), who wrote a widely read column in *Scientific American*.

Gertrude Mary Cox

January 13, 1900 – October 17, 1978

FARM LIFE

Gertrude Mary Cox grew up on a farm in a small town in Iowa. During her childhood, she and her three siblings did many farm chores. Gertrude loved to make bread. She admired her mother, who taught her the values of her church. This led Gertrude to dream of becoming a deaconess—a church official—as an adult.

RELIGION TO STATISTICS

After high school, Gertrude studied to become a deaconess, but after a few years, she realized she wanted to go to college to study mathematics. At Iowa State College in Ames, Gertrude was interested in more than just math, and she took classes in several other areas, including psychology. To make money, she worked in the computing laboratory, doing statistics calculations by hand, and fell in love with statistics. Gertrude worked hard to get a master's degree—her thesis was called *A Statistical Investigation of a Teacher's Ability as Indicated by the Success of His Students in Subsequent Courses.*

GRADUATE SCHOOL

After earning her master's degree, Gertrude moved to the University of California at Berkeley to get her PhD. While she was still studying for her PhD, George Snedecor offered her a job running the new Statistical Laboratory at Iowa State College. She decided to take the job instead of finishing her degree.

CONSIDER A WOMAN

Seven years later, in 1940, Frank Porter Graham, the president of North Carolina State College, was looking to create a department of experiment statistics. He asked Gertrude's boss, George, for a list of people he thought would be good professors in the new department. When George created a list of five men, Gertrude asked why her name hadn't been included. Although her question didn't cause George to add her to his list, he made a point of telling Frank, "If you would consider a woman, I know of no one better qualified than Gertrude M. Cox." This was how Gertrude got the job as head of the department. Her story is a good example of how asking for what you want might help you get it! In 1950, she wrote a book called *Experiment Designs*, which became the most referenced book in the field of statistics for many years.

BEING FIRST

Gertrude's work as a celebrated mathematician helped break down many gender barriers. She was the first female professor at North Carolina State College and later became an editor of the journal *Biometrics*. Gertrude was a founding member and later the president of the Biometrics Society. She was also a fellow and president of the American Statistical Association and the first female member of the Institute of Mathematical Statistics. She even had the honor of being elected to the National Academy of Sciences!

BARS, SHORT AND TALL

Gertrude Mary Cox was a great teacher who made it easy to understand statistics. In this activity, we'll learn how to easily present statistics using a bar graph.

MATERIALS

- At least 25 square LEGO bricks or other modular building blocks in at least six different colors
- Paper
- Pencil
- Ruler or straightedge
- A six-sided die

Fig. 7. Completed graph.

NOTE: LEGO®, the LEGO logo, and the Brick and Knob configurations are trademarks of the LEGO Group, which does not sponsor, authorize, or endorse this book.

DIRECTIONS

EXPERIMENT 1, COUNTING COLORS

1 Find at least twenty-five square LEGO bricks or other modular building blocks. Make sure you have at least six different colors. *Fig. 1.*

2 Stack all of the blocks of the same color into tall towers, like the bars in the graph of favorite colors from Ms. Coriander's class.

3 Stand the towers up next to each other on a flat surface. *Fig. 2.*

4 Your towers made a bar graph! Well done!

THE MATH IN THE FUN

A **bar graph** is a way of presenting data visually to make it easier to understand. It shows differences in data through the height of the bars, with taller bars representing more results in a category. Here's an example:

Imagine that Ms. Coriander has 26 students in her class and asks each what their favorite color is. Notice that turning the table data into a bar graph makes it easier to see the differences in how many students choose each color as their favorite.

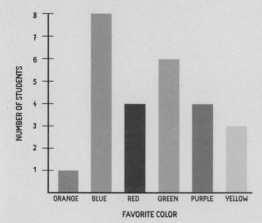

FAVORITE COLOR	NUMBER OF STUDENTS
Orange	1
Blue	8
Red	4
Green	6
Purple	4
Yellow	3

Fig. 1. Different colored piles of blocks.

Fig. 2. Example of a completed graph.

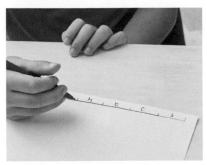

Fig. 3. Set up the graph background.

EXPERIMENT 2, COLLECTING DATA

1 On a piece of paper, using a pencil and ruler, draw a straight line at the bottom with the numbers 1 to 6. It should look like this. Make sure there is enough space between the numbers for your blocks. *Fig. 3*.

2 Roll a die. When you roll a number, place a block on that number. If you roll a number more than once, put the new block on top of the stack already at that number to make one tall bar. *Fig. 4* and *Fig. 5* and *Fig. 6* and *Fig. 7.*

- Try to keep all the blocks in each stack the same color.

- Try not to have two bars of the same color next to each other.

BONUS LEVEL

1 Repeat Experiment 2 again, but this time roll two dice instead of one and record the sum of the two dice. Hint: This time you will need the numbers 2 to 12 on the bottom of your bar graph. You may have to repeat colors, but this is okay as long as you keep the blocks above their individual numbers. (See below.)

2 Did you notice that some of the numbers from 2 to 12 occur more frequently than others? Can you figure out why this happens?

3 Try making a bar graph with the contents of a bag of M&M's, Skittles, or Smarties. Which color is the most common? Which is the rarest? Or use a bag with a mix of candies. Which types are the most and least common? The most important question is: Can you resist eating the candy until the experiment is over?

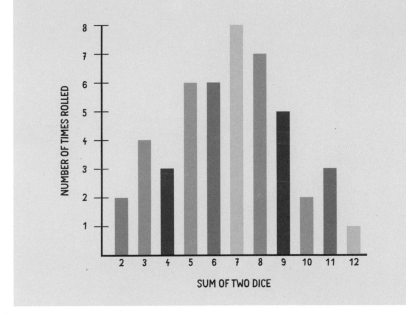

Fig. 4. A block on the space for number 6.

Fig. 5. A block added for the number 3.

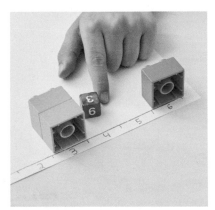

Fig. 6. Two blocks stacked on number 3.

Mary Cartwright

December 17, 1900 – April 3, 1998

HISTORY OR MATH?

As a young child, Mary Cartwright had a passion for history. However, during her final year before college, she discovered she was equally interested in studying math. Mary found she could do just as well in math as she had in history without having to spend time memorizing dates and events. So when she was accepted to Oxford University in England, she chose to study math.

TO UNIVERSITY AND BACK AGAIN

Mary worked extremely hard in college but didn't do as well as she had hoped. Feeling discouraged, she almost gave up on math in favor of returning to history. In the end, she decided she was still having fun studying math and continued with it. Following graduation, she taught at a couple of girls' schools before returning to Oxford to study for her doctorate. After earning her PhD in 1930, Mary received a fellowship to continue her research at Girton College, which is part of Cambridge University in England. While there, she attended lectures of J. E. Littlewood, who had been one of the examiners for her PhD defense. She solved an open problem he mentioned in a lecture with what is now known as Cartwright's theorem. Later, she was asked to become a lecturer at Cambridge. She was promoted to director of Studies in Mathematics at Girton in 1936.

THE "BUTTERFLY EFFECT"

In 1938, the Radio Research Board of the British Department of Scientific and Industrial Research published a set of questions that came out of their radio and radar work. Mary was interested but unfamiliar with the topic, so she approached Littlewood to collaborate on the new project. Together, they laid the foundations for a new branch of math called chaos theory and discovered what would later be called the "butterfly effect." The butterfly effect is the idea that very small changes can have giant effects. It was given that name because of Ray Bradbury's short story, *A Sound of Thunder*, in which a time traveler interacts with a butterfly in the past and changes the entire history of the world.

BREAKING GENDER BARRIERS

Dr. Mary Cartwright was a huge inspiration to female scholars. When she was accepted into Oxford, she was one of only five women studying math there. Mary later became the first woman to serve on the Council of the Royal Society, the first woman to receive the Sylvester Medal, and the first female president of the London Mathematical Society. She was honored by the queen and named Dame Mary Cartwright, Dame Commander of the Order of the British Empire. She was also the first woman to receive the De Morgan Medal, the London Mathematical Society's highest honor.

ORGANIZED CHAOS

Mary Cartwright studied chaos theory and here we'll do the same. In this activity, we will use water and food coloring to see what chaos theory looks like in action!

MATERIALS

- 1- or 2-cup (240 or 480 ml) measuring cup
- Water
- A medium waterproof container (bigger than a tissue box is preferable)
- Food coloring of your choice, preferably a dark color like blue, purple, or red
- An ice cube tray

DIRECTIONS

1 Measure out 2 cups (480 ml) of water into a container. Then add 3 to 6 drops of food coloring and mix it until the water is nice and dark. *Fig. 1* and *Fig. 2*.

2 Carefully pour the colored water into the ice cube tray. Then put the tray in the freezer overnight. *Fig. 3*.

3 Once the water has completely frozen into ice, fill the large container with hot water. The water should not be hot enough to burn you.

Fig. 5. Partially diffused.

Fig. 1. Measure 2 cups (480 ml).

Fig. 2. Add food coloring.

4 Take three ice cubes and drop them into the water in one corner of the container. They should all be in the same spot and hugging the corner as closely as possible. *Fig. 4*.

5 Slowly, you should see the food coloring leave the ice and disperse throughout the water. After a few hours, the entire container should be the exact same color throughout. *Fig. 5* and *Fig. 6*.

Fig. 3. Make ice cubes.

BONUS LEVEL

Think about it: What would happen if we used a tub of cold water and a small amount of colored hot water?

Can you think of other examples of chaos theory in your life?

Fig. 4. Add the colored ice to hot water.

THE MATH IN THE FUN

The cold water in the ice is slowly being warmed by the hot water around it. As the ice melts, food coloring is released into the larger container of water and randomly moves to places where there is less color until the color is completely evened out. This is called **diffusion**, the process by which a new substance becomes evenly distributed throughout a different substance. In this case, the food coloring will keep moving around until it is evenly dispersed throughout the water.

Fig. 6. Fully diffused.

STATISTICS

Florence Nightingale

May 12, 1820 – August 13, 1910

HIGH-SOCIETY CHILDHOOD

Florence Nightingale was born to wealthy parents who were part of England's elite social circles. However, Florence was not interested in climbing the social ladder. She wanted to help other people. By the time she was sixteen, Florence knew she wanted to be a nurse, but her parents were not supportive. Nursing was seen as a lower-class profession and Florence was expected to marry someone who would increase her family's social standing. However, she knew that if she married, she would have to focus on family instead of nursing, so when a man she liked proposed, she turned him down to follow her dreams.

FOLLOWING HER DREAMS

After finishing nursing school, Florence went to work at Harley Street Nursing Home in London. She did so well that she was offered a job as superintendent at the Institute for the Care of Sick Gentlewomen in London. When Florence noticed how cholera spread easily due to unsanitary conditions, she changed the institute's sanitation practices. It was hard work, but she succeeded, and far fewer people died as she fine-tuned her techniques.

TREATING THE SICK

A year after the Crimean War started, England was failing to treat thousands of hurt and dying soldiers. Florence assembled a group of the first thirty-four female nurses to help the soldiers in Crimea. She greatly reduced the number of deaths in the hospital by implementing sanitary practices and by taking care of the soldiers' other needs, including providing delicious food, books, and other improvements.

THE STATISTICS OF NURSING

Women of the time were frequently ignored, but Florence got people's attention by using statistics to back up her ideas. She even invented a new way of presenting data, called Nightingale rose diagrams, which made the data easy to understand! These circular graphs represented repeating sequences, such as the months in a year, with a continuous line to show how data changed as time went on. The data was shown by how far the line was from the center. If the line was further from the center, that meant the numbers were larger than if the line was closer to the center. She made another version of the diagram where the area of a wedge in the diagram represents change in data. These easy-to-understand representations of how sanitary improvements decreased death rates helped her convince others to adopt her practices.

LEGACY

Because she showed the world how persuasive statistics could be, Florence became the first female member of the Royal Statistical Society in England and an honorary member of the American Statistical Association. Her impact was so profound that she is often referred to as the creator of modern nursing. Her book, *Notes on Nursing: What It Is and What It Is Not*, is used to train nurses to this day. However, without her statistical ideas, she might not have been able to make her mark. Florence's story is a wonderful example of how math can make a monumental difference—in this case, by saving countless lives.

PIZZA PIE CHARTS

Florence Nightingale used diagrams on circles to present statistics in an easy-to-understand way. Here we will learn about another form of circular charts—pie charts!

NOTE: We strongly recommend that you do the Bars, Short and Tall activity associated with the Gertrude Mary Cox biography before doing this project.

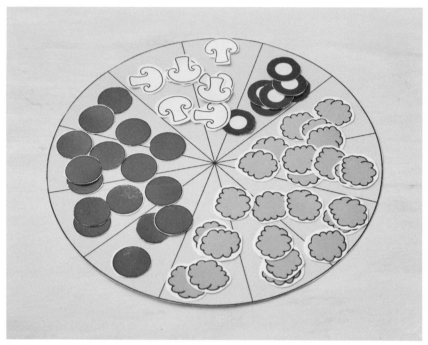

Fig. 5. A completed pizza!

THE MATH IN THE FUN

A **pie chart**, like a bar graph, is a visual way of representing data to make it easier for people to understand. Pie charts are good at representing **categorical data**, which is the data of groups. For example, looking back at Ms. Coriander's bar graph from the Bars, Short and Tall activity, each bar represented the number of people that preferred a color. We could make a pie chart to graph the same data. It would look like this (right).

Each color wedge shows what percentage of people prefer that color. The percentage of the wedge matches the percentage of people who prefer that color. A bigger wedge of the circle shows a greater number of students prefer that color. We can do the same thing with pizza toppings!

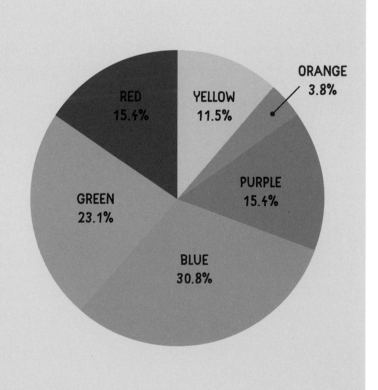

MATERIALS

- Scissors
- Pizza and toppings pullout from the back of the book (it can also be downloaded from www.mathlabforkids.com and https://quarto.com/files/MathForKids)
- Paper
- Pencil or pen

DIRECTIONS

EXPERIMENT 1

We did a survey of twelve people and gathered the following data:

- Five out of twelve people prefer cheese pizza.
- One-third of the people prefer pepperoni pizza.
- One-sixth of the people prefer mushroom pizza.
- One person prefers olive pizza.

1 With scissors, cut out the pizza and toppings from the pullout in the back of the book. It can also be downloaded from www.mathlabforkids.com and https://quarto.com/files/MathForKids.

2 We will use our data to cover the pizza in toppings, representing the fraction of people who prefer each topping. Beginning with cheese, use the cheese clouds to cover 5/12 of the pizza. Five sections should be covered in cheese and the slices should be next to each other. *Fig. 1.*

3 Next, add pepperoni to the pizza. First, figure out how many twelfths you need to make one-third. Once you figure that out, cover that many slices in pepperoni. *Fig. 2.*

Fig. 1. Pizza with cheese.

Fig. 2. Add pepperoni.

Fig. 3. Add mushrooms.

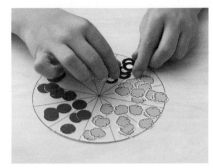
Fig. 4. Add olives.

4 For mushrooms, calculate how many twelfths equal one-sixth. Then cover that many slices in mushrooms. *Fig. 3.*

5 Finally, for olives, cover one slice. *Fig. 4.*

6 Now your pizza should look like this. *Fig. 5.*

EXPERIMENT 2

1 Take the toppings off your pizza pie chart so you can make another pie chart, but this time you collect the data! Ask your friends and family what their favorite pizza topping (out of cheese, pepperoni, mushrooms, and olives) is. Try to ask twelve people, but if you can't, only ask six.

2 Write down how many people prefer each topping and place the toppings on the pizza for each person. If you only asked six people, cover two slices per person.

NOTE: You may have zero people preferring one kind of topping. That is okay! Just don't place that topping on the pizza.

BONUS LEVEL

Use pizza toppings to represent other kinds of data, such as favorite colors. For example, imagine cheese represents yellow, pepperoni represents red, mushrooms represent blue, and olives represent green. Then try covering the pizza.

David Blackwell

April 24, 1919 – July 8, 2010

FAST EDUCATION

David Blackwell was brilliant, even as a child. He excelled so much in math that his teachers let him skip two grades in the subject, though it wasn't until high school that his true love for math began. David was so good at school, in fact, that he started college when he was only sixteen and won a scholarship to attend the University of Illinois at Urbana-Champaign. He intended to become a teacher but kept taking math classes because he loved math so much. David ended up earning a master's degree and a PhD by age twenty-two. Despite being a genius, his college experience was fairly normal. He even joined a fraternity!

DISCRIMINATION SETBACKS

David continued his impressive streak by earning a Rosenwald Fellowship, which would allow him to continue mathematical research after his PhD at the Institute for Advanced Study at Princeton University. However, because he was African American, David was prevented from doing research or attending classes at Princeton. This infuriated him, so he left the institute. He faced further discrimination when he was not hired at the University of California, Berkeley. Berkeley statistician Jerzy Neyman wanted to hire David, but he didn't get the job because the wife of the head of the mathematics department refused to allow a Black person into her house. Hoping to become a professor but worried his race would prevent him from doing so, David focused his job applications on historically Black colleges and universities. He made a name for himself at Howard University, becoming head of the mathematics department after working there for only three years.

STATISTICAL STUDIES

While David was working at Howard University, he met Meyer A. Gershick. Meyer introduced him to the field of statistics and David's interest grew deeper as the two became friends. They studied game theory as well, applying it to the military and battlefields for the RAND Corporation. Together, they wrote and published *Theory of Games and Statistical Decisions*. David continued studying statistics on his own, combining it with his love of teaching to write *Basic Statistics*, one of the first textbooks on Bayesian statistics. He didn't limit his research to statistics. He also studied the field of probability. While probability and statistics are related, they are not the same. Probability tries to figure out how likely things are to happen, whereas statistics tries to determine relationships based on data.

BREAKING BARRIERS

Despite originally being turned down for a job at Berkeley due to his race, in 1954 Dr. David Blackwell was offered an opportunity to work there as a visiting professor. A year later, he became a full professor in Berkeley's new statistics department and was made department chair the following year. In addition to being the first tenured African American faculty member at Berkeley, David continued breaking down racial barriers as the first African American inducted into the National Academy of Sciences. Over his career, David won numerous honors and awards and was an inspiration to other mathematicians.

ALWAYS BET ON MATH

David Blackwell used probability and statistics to study games. We're going to play a betting game and use probability to help us win as often as we can.

MATERIALS

- 2 players
- 2 dice
- At least 30 small tokens, coins, or candies
- A bowl

RULES OF THE GAME

1 Players 1 and 2 both start with a die and an equal number of tokens, coins, or candies. (These are the "money" in the game.) *Fig. 1.*

2 Player 1 picks four numbers between 2 and 12. *Fig. 2.*

3 Players 1 and 2 make a bet on whether one of those numbers will turn up on the dice. Player 1 bets that one of their numbers will turn up, and Player 2 bets that they won't. Each player places at least one of their tokens into the bowl. The bowl is called "the pot." *Fig. 3.*

Fig. 5. The winner gets the money!

DIRECTIONS

1 Players 1 and 2 roll their dice and find the sum of the face-up numbers. If the sum equals one of the numbers Player 1 chose, Player 1 takes the pot. If the sum is any of the other numbers, Player 2 gets the pot. *Fig. 4 and Fig 5.*

2 The players make new bets and continue to play until one person has all the money!

Which player do you prefer to be, Player 1 or Player 2? Player 2 wins on a larger number of numbers, but if Player 1 picks their numbers in a smart way, could they have a better chance of winning. Once you think you have figured it out, move on to the Math in the Fun.

BONUS LEVEL

What if Player 1 could choose four numbers OR draw six random numbers? With eleven possible numbers, six is more than half of the total. But are the odds better if you are choosing four numbers or taking six randomly?

Fig. 1. Start with equal tokens.

Fig. 2. Player 1 picks four numbers.

Fig. 3. Make your bets.

Fig. 4. Roll the dice.

THE MATH IN THE FUN

It is better to be Player 1! If you pick the most common numbers, you'll have a better chance of winning, even with fewer numbers. There are multiple sets of four numbers that give you a greater than 50 percent chance of winning. One good set is the numbers 5, 6, 7, and 8. See if you can figure out why, and also figure out some other good sets.

HINT: Draw a sum table. In a sum table, each box contains the sum of the row and column it's in.

	1	2	3	4	5	6
1	Example: 1+1=2					
2					Example: 5+2=7	
3						
4						
5						
6				Example: 4+6=10		

Nalini Joshi

Born: 1958

GROWING UP IN MYANMAR

Nalini Joshi was born in Myanmar (also known as Burma), where she lived while she was young. A decade after her father was forced to join the army, the family immigrated to Australia. Nalini recalls that they faced possible imprisonment if they ever returned to Myanmar. Even now, she has mixed feelings on visiting her old home. After moving to Australia, Nalini fell in love with books and science.

APPLIED MATH

Even before her career properly started, Nalini was so impressive that she earned the University Medal for her bachelor's degree in applied mathematics from the University of Sydney in Australia. She then went to Princeton University in the United States for her PhD in applied and computational mathematics. Applied math uses mathematical ideas and approaches to solve problems in science, engineering, and other areas. It also creates and improves problem-solving methods in those areas. Nalini focuses on solving problems from the natural world using pure and applied math. Many of her papers have influenced physics and wireless communications. Nalini became the chair of applied mathematics at the University of Sydney in 2002, making her the first female math professor at the university. She has also been the director of the University of Sydney's Centre for Mathematical Biology and head of their School of Mathematics and Statistics.

SPEAKING UP FOR EQUALITY

Nalini has long been an advocate for gender equality. She cofounded and cochaired the Science in Australia Gender Equity (SAGE) program to improve gender equity in Australian higher education and research. She has given many talks discussing the lack of female representation in mathematics and STEM (science, technology, engineering, and math). Nalini says, "In addition to long-standing interests in mathematics research and education, I have a particular interest in increasing the participation of women and minority groups in science and mathematics." Her efforts to further gender equality were celebrated when her portrait was hung alongside many other famous University of Sydney professors on International Women's Day in 2017.

RECOGNITION

Dr. Nalini Joshi's mathematical success and equity efforts have been honored in many ways. She was the first Australian to be elected vice president of the International Mathematical Union. She received the Eureka Prize for Outstanding Mentor of Young Researchers, was appointed an Officer of the Order of Australia, and has been president of the Australian Mathematical Society. Nalini also won the Australian Mathematical Society's George Szekeres Medal for sustained outstanding contribution to the mathematical sciences. She used winning the Szekeres Medal as a teaching opportunity, noting, "When I went to check the list of past winners, I was surprised to see that I am the first person of color on the list."

LOVING MATH

Nalini firmly believes that math is not only beautiful, but also incredibly fun! She is quite active on Twitter, where she often posts about how beautiful math is. Once, she even tweeted, "Maths is in my heart." She uses her media presence to further her fight for equality and promote a wider understanding of math for everyone.

THE THREE BOXES PROBLEM

Nalini Joshi teaches applied mathematics. In this game, we'll apply math, specifically probability and statistics, to give us the best chance of winning sweet treats!

MATERIALS

- 3 small boxes, bowls, or buckets
- A small prize like candy
- 2 people
- Your brain!

DIRECTIONS

There are three boxes. Two of them are empty and one of them is filled with candy (or another prize). The problem is, you don't know which box has the candy and which boxes are empty. Your friend tells you to pick one and you'll get to keep whatever's inside. You choose, but before you open the box, your friend opens one of the other boxes and it's empty. Now your friend says you can change your mind and pick the other closed box if you want. Should you change boxes or stick with the one you originally chose?

1 Decide who is the host and who is the contestant. The contestant leaves the room.

2 While the contestant is in a different room, the host hides the prize completely inside one of the boxes and arranges them in a line. *Fig. 1.*

Fig. 6. The winner gets the prize.

3 The host tells the contestant to come back into the room when they are done setting up the boxes.

4 The contestant picks a box that they think contains the prize. *Fig. 2.*

5 The host picks up a different box, one that does not have the prize under it, revealing that it is not the box with the prize. *Fig. 3.*

6 The contestant then decides whether they want to keep their choice of box or pick the box the host didn't reveal. *Fig. 4.*

7 The contestant picks up the box they chose in the previous step. If they find the prize, they keep it! *Fig. 5.*

8 The winner gets the prize. *Fig. 6.*

Fig. 1. Host sets up the boxes.

Fig. 2. Contestant chooses a box.

Fig. 3. Host reveals an empty box.

Fig. 4. Contestant chooses again.

Fig. 5. The reveal!

BONUS LEVEL

Try playing again, switching who is the host and who is the contestant until you figure out whether it's better to keep the box you first chose or switch boxes. Once you have a guess about whether it's better to keep or switch boxes, read the Math in the Fun for the answer.

THE MATH IN THE FUN

The Three Boxes Problem is a version of the famous Monty Hall Problem, which works the same way. There has been a long-standing debate around whether to switch or stick with your original choice, but using probability we can figure out which choice truly gives you the best chance of winning. Many people think that it doesn't matter, since there are two boxes at the end and one of them has the prize. Some people believe you have a 50 percent chance of winning whether or not you switch. However, if we use probability, we see that's not true. When you first pick a box, you have a one-third chance of it being the right box and a two-thirds chance of one of the other boxes having the prize. When one box is revealed to be empty, the odds don't change. After one empty box is revealed, you know that the other box you didn't choose has a two-thirds chance of containing the prize. So we can give ourselves the best chance of winning by switching boxes.

Persi Diaconis

Born: January 31, 1945

THE MATHEMAGICIAN

When Persi Diaconis was fourteen years old, he dropped out of high school and ran away from home to travel with Dai Vernon, a world-class magician. Persi became a professional magician, performing all over the world for more than a decade. One of the things he loved about magic was the math behind some of his tricks. Eventually, Persi decided to go back to school and began studying math at City College of New York, where he got his bachelor's degree. Later, the head of Harvard's statistics department, who was also a mathemagician (mathematical magician), arranged for Persi to get into Harvard's PhD program. Persi has been a math and statistics professor at either Harvard or Stanford ever since.

CARD SHUFFLING

Persi's mathematical interests include randomness and randomization, especially coin flipping and card shuffling. One of his most famous papers investigated how many times a normal fifty-two-card deck needs to be riffle (standard) shuffled to be considered truly randomized. The paper proved that a deck should be shuffled seven times, and that more shuffles wouldn't introduce much extra randomness. More than a decade after publishing that paper, a company that makes card-shuffling machines used by casinos asked Persi to check whether their machines were randomizing the decks enough. It turned out that the machines weren't shuffling well enough, so it's a good thing they asked Persi to check! The mathematics of card shuffling has applications to turbulence, fluid dynamics, and even how long a vat of cookie dough must be blended to make sure the ingredients are mixed enough.

FLIPPING COINS

Persi has also investigated whether a coin flip is as fair as we think. He found out that a flipped coin is more likely to end up on the same side on which it starts. But he is quick to point out that the coin will only land on the same side about 51 percent of the time, so flipping a coin is still pretty close to fair. That said, you should never agree to flip a coin with Persi, as he has practiced so much that he can flip a coin to come up heads ten times in a row!

DIACONIS THE DEBUNKER

Persi is a well-known skeptic. He famously debunked some prominent psychics who claimed to be experts in extrasensory perception (also known as ESP or sixth sense). Persi believes he is in a better position than most to figure out what is really going on when someone is supposedly practicing telepathy or bending spoons with their mind. Magicians, like psychics, use many psychological tricks, so Persi can better spot them in use. Also, his deep understanding of statistics helps him know when someone is using statistics in a sloppy or intentionally deceptive way.

HONORS AND AWARDS

Persi Diaconis won the MacArthur Fellowship (often called the "genius prize") in 1982. He and Ron Graham (whom you can also read about in this book) wrote a book called *Magical Mathematics: The Mathematical Ideas That Animate Great Magic Tricks*. The book won the Euler Book Prize for "an outstanding book in mathematics that is likely to improve the public view of the field." Persi is very proud to be a member of the National Academy of Sciences, American Philosophical Society, and American Academy of Arts and Sciences.

MATHEMATICAL MAGIC

Did you know that many of the magic tricks magicians do are based on math? Here you'll learn how to amaze your friends with mathematical magic, just like Persi Diaconis does!

MATERIALS

- A full deck of 52 cards

DIRECTIONS

1 Give your audience a pile of nine cards from your deck.

2 Tell your audience, "Here's a small pile of cards. Pick one, memorize it, then put it on top of the others in a small stack." *Fig. 1.*

3 Shuffle the deck, keeping the nine cards from the audience's pile on the bottom in the same order they gave you the cards. In our example, the ace of diamonds was the chosen card. You can see it is on top of the small pile. When you perform the trick, make sure it is facedown. We only put it faceup in our example so you can see it. *Fig. 2.*

OPTIONAL: Feel free to tell your audience you aren't good at shuffling but that it doesn't really matter. Then you can pretend to shuffle. The only thing that matters is making sure the pile of nine cards you gave them remains on the bottom.

Fig. 1. The audience's card.

Fig. 2. The audience's card on top of the pile at the bottom of the deck.

4 Now comes the tricky part! Tell your audience you're going to count down from ten, flipping over a top card each time, and if the card number matches the number you say, you'll stop making your pile. Kings, queens, and jacks are worth ten while aces are worth one.

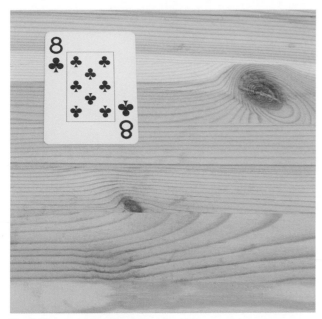

Fig. 3. First card flipped.

Fig. 4. Nine is the number you said.

Fig. 5. Start a new pile.

Fig. 6. End of the second pile.

EXAMPLE: First you say, "Ten!" and flip over a card. Here it is an eight. Eight is not ten, the number you said, so you continue. If the card had been a king, queen, jack, or ten, you would have stopped. *Fig. 3.*

Next, you say, "Nine!" and flip over a card. It is a nine! Since the card you flipped is the same as the number you said, your pile is done! *Fig. 4.*

5 You'll make a total of four piles. If you count all the way down to one without a match, put one last card on top of the pile facedown.

EXAMPLE: Here in the second pile you drew a three, so you keep flipping. When you say nine, you draw a ten, then you draw a king when you say eight and a queen when you say seven. The sixth card is a four and the fifth card is a seven, but when you said "Four!" you flipped another four! This means your second pile is done and you start the third pile. *Fig. 5* and *Fig. 6.*

project continues ▶

Fig. 7. Pile with no matches.

Fig. 8. Cap the pile.

EXAMPLE: In the next pile, you never draw the number you say. So at the end, place a card face-down on top of the pile. The fourth pile also has no match, so you place a card on top of it too. At the end, these are your four piles and what is left of your deck. *Fig. 7* and *Fig. 8* and *Fig. 9.*

6 Now add up the numbers that are faceup on your four piles. Then draw that many cards. The last card you reveal will be the audience's chosen card!

EXAMPLE: The cards we see faceup are the nine and the four: 9 + 4 = 13, so we draw twelve cards and reveal the thirteenth. It is the ace of diamonds, the audience's card! *Fig. 10.*

NOTE: If all four piles need a card on top, instead of placing a card on top of the fourth pile, reveal that card. It is your audience's card.

Fig. 9. Four piles and the deck.

Fig. 10. The ace of diamonds. It worked!

BONUS LEVEL

Try to figure out how this trick works!

- Hint 1: Why does it matter that the card is ninth from the bottom?

- Hint 2: Count how many cards each pile makes you draw.

If you figured it out, see if you can do a similar trick with a different number of cards.

THE MATH IN THE FUN

Magic tricks are often based on mathematics. For those who don't know that math is happening, math often looks like magic! We can use our knowledge of math to make it look like what we're doing is impossible. In the trick above, our math is based on addition and subtraction, but there are plenty of other tricks based on other kinds of math. For example, there is a magic trick Persi talks about in his book that involves cutting a deck of four cards repeatedly that looks like it randomly mixes up the cards, but actually, one particular card will always come out on top. This trick is based on some trickier math, and is super cool!

George Boole

November 2, 1815 – December 8, 1864

WORKING YOUNG

George Boole grew up in a very loving but poor family. His father, John Boole, was a member of the Lincoln Mechanics' Institute, a group that helped working men further their education. John passed his love of learning and books on to George, who also joined the group. Unfortunately, because his father wasn't very successful in his career, George had to start working at age sixteen to help support his parents and siblings. He got a junior teacher job in Doncaster, England.

CREATING A SCHOOL

George's first job didn't pay enough for him to provide for his family, so when he was nineteen, he decided to open his own school in Lincoln. George was an excellent head of school with strong leadership and teaching abilities. Four years later, his great reputation placed him in a position to take over a bigger school in Waddington.

BECOMING A MATH PROFESSOR

Even during his early career running schools and teaching, George made time to study math. He could read multiple languages, which allowed him to read many math books and papers. Mathematician Duncan F. Gregory, who had a more intensive math research education and was the editor of the *Cambridge Mathematical Journal*, became a good friend and mentor to George, despite being only two years older. Duncan taught George how to write a mathematical paper, allowing George to publish his first math paper in 1840. Publishing math papers led to George becoming the first professor of mathematics at Queen's College, Cork in Ireland in 1849. Finally, George was able to fulfill his dream of studying math full-time while still earning enough money to provide for his family.

MATHEMATICAL FAMILY

While working as a professor, George met Mary Everest (whom you can also read about in this book), the niece of one of his colleagues. The two of them became very close and eventually married. Together they had five daughters. Sadly, George died of pneumonia shortly after the birth of their fifth daughter. Their daughters had amazing careers too, many following in the footsteps of their parents to become academics. One of their children, Alicia Boole Stott, even became a respected mathematician in the field of four-dimensional geometry!

BOOLEAN LOGIC

George is best known for inventing Boolean logic, also known as Boolean algebra. His innovation was to apply methods from the then-new field of symbolic algebra to logic. Over two thousand years earlier, the famous philosopher Aristotle had laid out rules of logic. George wanted to broaden the rules so they would be useful in more situations and give it a solid mathematical foundation. As is often the case in mathematics, George pursued this work because it was interesting, despite the fact that there were no obvious practical applications. Nearly a hundred years later, mathematician Claude Shannon, who is commonly called "the father of information theory," realized that Boolean algebra could optimize telephone routing switches. Using electrical switches to process logic is the fundamental concept underlying all modern computers!

THE PRINCESS'S PUZZLES

Did you know that puzzles are extremely mathematical? Well, they are, and here we'll explore a special kind—logic puzzles! They have tricky solutions and are super fun to solve.

MATERIALS

- A piece of paper
- A pencil

DIRECTIONS

PUZZLE 1

The princess's dog, Fluffy, was kidnapped! Fluffy is a special dog with purple polka dots and golden eyes. The guards have swept the city and found five dogs matching Fluffy's description. The problem is that each dog has a child claiming the dog is theirs. Each child—Aaliyah, Bo, Imani, Jaiden, and Marissa—has given a statement. The four who actually own a purple polka-dotted dog with golden eyes all told the truth, and the one who kidnapped the princess's dog lied. If four are telling the truth and one is lying, figure out who kidnapped Fluffy. Here is what each child said:

Aaliyah: "Bo and I got our dogs together three years ago."

Bo: "Marissa didn't kidnap Fluffy."

Imani: "Aaliyah is telling the truth."

Jaiden: "I didn't kidnap Fluffy."

Marissa: "I just adopted my dog; her name is Spot."

HOW TO SOLVE

Let's make a table.

If Aaliyah is lying, the other children would be telling the truth. Is this possible? Check off the names of the people in Aaliyah's row who could tell the truth if she is lying.

Fill out each row of the table, assuming that the kid named in that row is lying.

Move on to the next page, once you're done, for the answer.

	Does Aaliyah's statement make sense?	Does Bo's statement make sense?	Does Imani's statement make sense?	Does Jaiden's statement make sense?	Does Marissa's statement make sense?	Does this work?
If Aaliyah is lying...						
If Bo is lying...						
If Imani is lying...						
If Jaiden is lying...						
If Marissa is lying...						

Did you figure out who the liar is?

Here is how we thought about it: We know that one of the children is lying and the rest are telling the truth. What happens if we assume Aaliyah is lying?

If Aaliyah is lying, then she kidnapped Fluffy and all the other kids are telling the truth. That means Bo is correct, and it wasn't Marissa, which makes sense given what Marissa said. Jaiden simply said it wasn't him, and that works if Aaliyah is the liar. But there is a problem with Imani's statement. Imani says Aaliyah is telling the truth, but if she is the liar, that means Imani is lying too! That doesn't fit the rules of the puzzle, so Aaliyah can't be the liar.

Okay, so what if Bo is the liar? Bo said that Marissa didn't kidnap Fluffy, but if Bo is lying, then Marissa is the dognapper. Why, then, would Bo lie? So Bo must be telling the truth. Since Bo is telling the truth, Marissa must be too, since Bo said she didn't kidnap Fluffy.

That just leaves two options for the liar: Imani and Jaiden. Imani says Aaliyah is telling the truth, and since we know she must be, that means Imani can't be lying. That only leaves Jaiden, so Jaiden must be the dognapper!

Here's how we filled out the logic table to help us crack the case.

	Does Aaliyah's statement make sense?	Does Bo's statement make sense?	Does Imani's statement make sense?	Does Jaiden's statement make sense?	Does Marissa's statement make sense?	Does this work?
If Aaliyah is lying...		Yes!	Imani must be lying too	Yes!	Yes!	Doesn't work
If Bo is lying...	Yes!		Yes!	Yes!	Marissa must be lying too	Doesn't work
If Imani is lying...	Aliyah must be lying too	Yes!		Yes!	Yes!	Doesn't work
If Jaiden is lying...	Yes!	Yes!	Yes!		Yes!	Works!
If Marissa is lying...	Yes!	Bo must be lying too	Yes!	Yes!		Doesn't work

BONUS LEVEL

The princess needs your help again! Her old lab partner ruined their entire model volcano so now the princess wants to find a new lab partner. Her sister recommends one of the Emeraldi brothers, three princes from a nearby kingdom. The brothers also have a sister who warns the princess that her oldest brother always tells the truth and the youngest brother always lies. The middle brother sometimes lies and sometimes tells the truth. The princess can ask one of the brothers one question before she makes her choice, but she won't know which brother she is asking the question. The princess decides that the one who always tells the truth would be best, but the liar would be okay too because she could at least always figure out what the truth is. The only brother the princess really doesn't want as her lab partner is the one that sometimes lies and sometimes tells the truth. What question can she ask to guarantee she picks a brother that always tells the truth or always lies? You can find the answer in the Hints and Solutions section in the back of the book.

THE MATH IN THE FUN

Logic puzzles are awesome and show up everywhere! Games like Sudoku and KenKen, for example, are logic puzzles. Logic puzzles usually have a trick to them, and often require eliminating false answers or finding patterns for smaller examples. For more puzzle fun, see if you can create your own puzzle or find more online to solve!

$$\frac{d}{dt}\left(\sum_{a} \frac{\delta L}{\delta \frac{dq_a}{dt}} \delta q_a\right) = 0$$

Emmy Noether

March 23, 1882 – April 14, 1935

TRAILBLAZER

When Amalie Emmy Noether died, Albert Einstein wrote in the *New York Times* that she was widely considered to be the greatest female mathematician who had ever lived. Emmy earned her PhD in 1907 from the University of Erlangen in Germany, where she was one of only two women enrolled. After she graduated, Emmy taught at Erlangen for seven years without being paid or having an official title.

CONTROVERSY

In 1915, two famous mathematicians, David Hilbert and Felix Klein, invited Emmy to join the math department at the University of Göttingen, one of the best math and physics research centers in the world at that time. Various nonmath professors objected to a woman joining the faculty, but David famously responded to the controversy by saying, "I do not see that the sex of the candidate is an argument against her [being a professor]. After all, we are a university, not a bath house." Nevertheless, Emmy was not allowed to officially join the faculty, so she spent four years teaching at the University of Göttingen by pretending to be David's assistant.

NOETHER'S FIRST FAMOUS THEOREM

In 1918, Emmy proved what remains today one of the most important theorems in physics! The theorem, which is called Noether's theorem, states, "Wherever a symmetry of nature exists, there is a conservation law attached to it, and vice versa." Conservation of momentum, also known as Newton's third law, and general relativity are both examples of Noether's theorem.

MORE GROUNDBREAKING WORK

Finally, in 1919, Emmy was allowed to teach under her own name. She quickly became one of the leading members of the Göttingen math department. Her students were sometimes called "Noether boys." In the second phase of her career, her work changed and guided abstract algebra, an important field of mathematics. In the final chapter of her influential career, Emmy united the previously separate mathematical fields of representation theory and the theory of modules and ideals, which allowed both fields to progress further than they had separately.

UNUSUAL TEACHING STYLE

Unlike most professors, Dr. Emmy Noether did not develop lesson plans but used lecture time to discuss important math questions with her students. Some of her students took very careful notes, which ended up being important, as many of Emmy's most significant ideas were developed during her lectures. A few of her students even turned their detailed notes into influential textbooks. Teaching was so important to Emmy that she sometimes held classes at her home when the university was closed and once took a class to a coffee shop to deliver a lecture on a holiday. Emmy was extremely generous and sometimes allowed her students or colleagues to take credit for her ideas to help their careers.

MOVE TO THE UNITED STATES

In 1933, Germany's Nazi government fired all Jews from university jobs, forcing Emmy and many other famous scholars to flee. Emmy was so well known that she received a grant to move to Bryn Mawr College in the United States. She also taught at the Institute for Advanced Study at Princeton but didn't feel welcome at "the men's university, where nothing female is admitted." On the other hand, she treasured her time at Bryn Mawr, where she had many enthusiastic female collaborators.

FABULOUS FOLDING FLEXAGONS

Flexagons are interesting shapes that can be folded and bent to reveal previously hidden aspects. In this activity, we'll make a trihexaflexagon, which is a shape that looks like a hexagon but has three sides!

MATERIALS

- Trihexaflexagon template from the back of the book (it can also be downloaded from www.mathlabforkids.com and https://quarto.com/files/MathForKids)

- Paper (thicker paper or cardstock works best but any paper will do)

- Craft knife (recommended) or scissors

- Cutting mat and ruler (if using a craft knife)

- Colored pencils or markers (optional)

- Pencil

- Tape

DIRECTIONS

CONSTRUCT A TRIHEXAFLEXAGON

1 Copy the Trihexaflexagon template from the book. You'll get best results with thicker paper or cardstock. (It can also be downloaded from www.mathlabforkids.com and https://quarto.com/files/MathForKids.)

2 With craft knife or scissors, cut out the template. If desired, color all the 1s one color, the 2s a second color, and the 3s a third color. *Fig. 1.*

Fig. 12. "Open up" the flexagon.

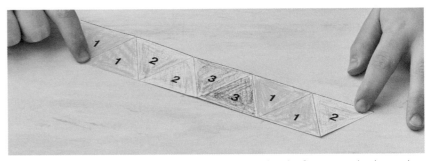

Fig. 1. Cut out the template and color all the 1s one color, the 2s a second color, and the 3s a third color.

3 Carefully fold along all the lines in both directions. It is important to crease each fold in both directions. If you have a craft knife, you'll get best results if you have an adult very lightly score along each line using a ruler to keep the lines straight.

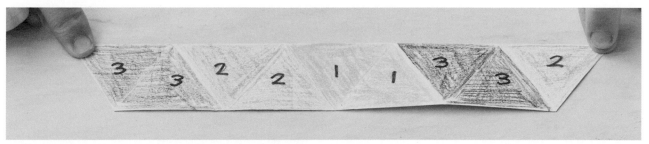

Fig. 2. Label the triangles on the back 3-3-2-2-1-1-3-3-2 from left to right.

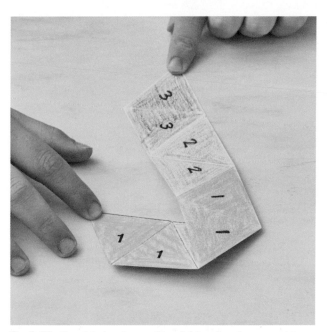

Fig. 3. Flip the strip back over, then fold so four 1s are next to each other.

Fig. 4. Fold the strip so you can see all six 1s with the 2 on top.

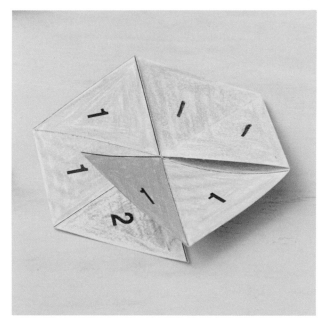

Fig. 5. Tuck the triangle labeled 2 behind the triangle labeled 1.

4 Turn the strip around and label the triangles 3-3-2-2-1-1-3-3-2 from left to right. Make sure the leftmost 3 has a 2 on the other side and the right-most 2 has a 1 on its other side. If you colored the triangles in step 2, use the same colors for the numbers you used on the other side. The second part of the template shows you the order to label the other side too. *Fig. 2.*

5 Flip the strip back over to the printed side, then fold so that you have four 1s next to each other. *Fig. 3.*

6 Fold the strip so that you can see all six 1s with the 2 on top. *Fig. 4.*

7 Tuck the triangle labeled 2 behind the triangle labeled 1 that would otherwise be below it. *Fig. 5.*

project continues ▶

8 Tape the top of the triangle labeled 1 to the triangle labeled 2 that is tucked behind it. *Fig. 6.*

9 You will now have all 1s on the front and all 3s on the back. *Fig. 7* and *Fig. 8.*

Fig. 6. Tape the top of the triangle labeled 1 to the triangle labeled 2 that is tucked behind.

Fig. 7. All 1s on the front.

Fig. 8. All 3s on the back.

BONUS LEVEL

Once you get the hang of making and flexing trihexaflexagons, you can decorate them to make them even more interesting. Try drawing a circle around the center of a face and then flexing. Something neat will happen.

THE MATH IN THE FUN

Many of Emmy's contributions were to an area of math called abstract algebra, which studies mathematical objects called groups, rings, and fields. One of the simplest types of groups is called a **cyclic group**. In a cyclic group, every element of the group can be made by repeatedly applying the group operation to one of the elements. Our trihexaflexagon demonstrates this process. You start with the side with all 1s, and then flex it to get the side with all 2s, and then flex it to get the side with all 3s. If you flex one more time, you'll get back to the side with all 1s and you can keep going forever in a cycle. Or if you start from the other side, you will cycle through 3s, then 2s, then 1s, then back to 3s again.

FLEX YOUR TRIHEXAFLEXAGON

1 Now comes the fun part: flexing! Push the creases between the two 1s you labeled by hand and the other two adjacent 1s all toward each other. *Fig. 9* and *Fig. 10.*

2 Pull the tips of the tops of the triangles out from the center. *Fig. 11* and *Fig. 12* (on page 100).

3 You have now revealed the third face of the trihexaflexagon! *Fig. 13.*

4 You can repeat steps 1 and 2 as often as you want to cycle through all three faces. If after pushing in all the creases as in step 1, the shape won't open up as in step 2, try pushing in a different set of adjacent triangles instead.

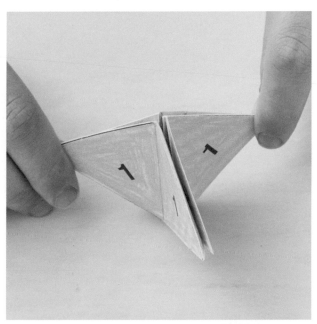

Fig. 9. Push in the crease between the hand-labeled 1s.

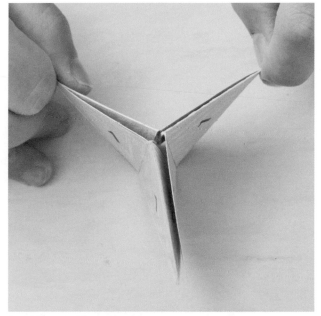

Fig. 10. Push in the other creases.

Fig. 11. Pull out the tips of the tops.

Fig. 13. Reveal the third face!

Martin Gardner

October 21, 1914 – May 22, 2010

MATH POPULARIZER

Martin Gardner never took a college math class and didn't consider himself a mathematician. Despite that, mathematicians proudly claim Martin as one of their own because he did more than anyone else in the twentieth century (and maybe ever) to popularize and explain math to nonmathematicians. Persi Diaconis (also featured in this book) joked, "Warning: Martin Gardner has turned dozens of innocent youngsters into math professors and thousands of math professors into innocent youngsters." Martin hung out with some of the most famous people of the twentieth century—writers, artists, Nobel Prize winners, world-famous magicians, and, of course, mathematicians.

MATHEMATICAL GAMES

Martin started as a writer/editor of children's magazines and particularly enjoyed paper-folding puzzles. He once wrote a column for *Scientific American* (*SA*), a widely read popular science magazine, about hexaflexagons. That column was such a success that the editor asked, "Is there enough similar material . . . to make a regular feature?" The answer was a resounding yes! For twenty-five years, Martin wrote a monthly column in *SA* called "Mathematical Games." Many famous scientists, such as Albert Einstein, have written articles for *SA*, but Martin's column was the magazine's most popular section for many years. His column was so widely read that he sometimes made people famous just by writing about them. For example, M. C. Escher, now one of the twentieth century's most famous artists, was basically unknown until Martin included his work in a column. (You can read more about Escher's work in the section on Jennifer McLoud-Mann.)

MARTIN THE MAGICIAN

Martin was fascinated by magic. His first publication, when he was only fifteen years old, was a magic trick in the official magazine of the Society of American Magicians. He helped pay his University of Chicago tuition by performing magic tricks at a department store. Martin's book *The Encyclopedia of Impromptu Magic* is highly respected among magicians and his book about mathematical magic tricks, *Mathematics, Magic, and Mystery*, is still a classic. *Magic* magazine recognized Martin as one of the "100 Most Influential Magicians of the Twentieth Century." Fittingly, his last published article was also a magic trick.

SKEPTIC

Martin was a famous skeptic of all forms of pseudoscience. He is credited with launching the modern skeptical movement with his book *Fads and Fallacies in the Name of Science*. The famed evolutionary biologist and history of science writer Stephen Jay Gould called Martin "The Quack Detector" who "expunged nonsense [and was] a priceless national resource."

OTHER WRITING

Martin wrote or edited more than a hundred books and countless articles, columns, and reviews. In addition to books and articles on math, magic, and skepticism, he wrote two novels. Martin's most famous and best-selling book, which sold over a million copies, was *The Annotated Alice*. It included the original illustrations and entire text of Lewis Carroll's *Alice's Adventures in Wonderland* and *Through the Looking-Glass*, along with extensive commentary explaining mathematical concepts, wordplay, literary references, games, and customs of the time in which Carroll wrote the books. Academics had been writing annotated versions of books meant to be read by other scholars for a long time, but *The Annotated Alice* was the first annotated book aimed at all readers. It was such a success that it spawned a whole field of annotated books written for the general public. Martin wrote several more, including annotated versions of famous poems "Casey at the Bat" and "The Night Before Christmas."

A HEAP OF HEXAGONS

We'll make an object that will look just like the trihexaflexagons we made earlier but it has six sides instead of three!

NOTE: We strongly recommend you do the Fabulous Folding Flexagons activity before you do this one.

MATERIALS

- Hexahexaflexagon template from the back of the book (it can also be downloaded from www.mathlabforkids.com and https://quarto.com/files/MathForKids)
- Paper
- Craft knife (recommended) or scissors
- Cutting mat and ruler (if using a craft knife)
- Colored pencils or markers (optional)
- Glue stick

DIRECTIONS

1 Copy the template from the book onto paper. It can also be downloaded from www.mathlabforkids.com and https://quarto.com/files/MathForKids.

2 With a craft knife or scissors, cut out the template. If desired, color all the 1s one color, the 2s a second color, and the 3s a third color. The nineteenth triangle doesn't have a number on it because it won't be visible in the final hexahexaflexagon, so there is no need to color it. *Fig. 1.*

Fig. 9. All six 2s are visible, with 3 on top.

3 Carefully fold along all the lines in both directions. It is important to crease each fold in both directions. If you have a craft knife, you'll get best results if you have an adult very lightly score along each line using a ruler to keep the lines straight.

4 Flip the strip over. This side will have the first triangle blank instead of the last. The rest will be labeled 4-4-5-5-6-6 from left to right repeated three times. Make sure the blank triangle on this side has a 1 on the other side. Make sure the blank triangle on the other side has a 6 on this side. The last part of the template shows you the order to label the other side. If you colored the triangles in step 2, use three new colors for this side so you are using a total of six colors. *Fig. 2.*

5 Wind the long strip around itself to make a shorter strip by having the back numbers face their partner. Fold the first 4 to face the second 4. *Fig. 3* and *Fig. 4.*

6 Fold the first 5 to face the second 5. *Fig. 5.*

7 Fold the first 6 to face the second 6.

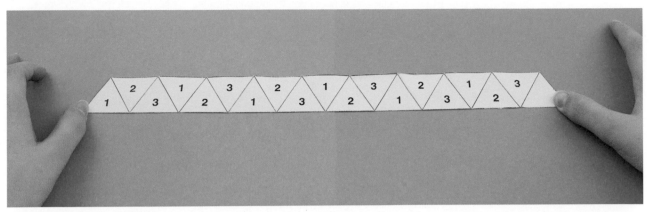

Fig. 1. The front of the template.

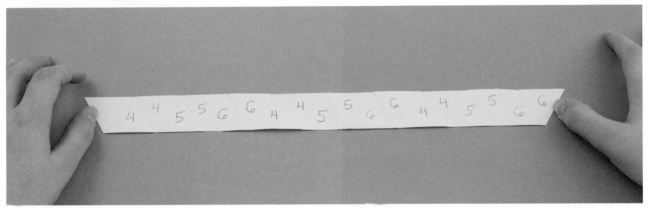

Fig. 2. Label the back with the 4-4-5-5-6-6 pattern.

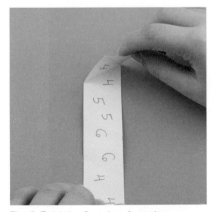

Fig. 3. Fold the first 4 to face the second 4.

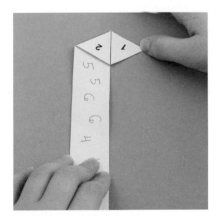

Fig. 4. The 4s folded together.

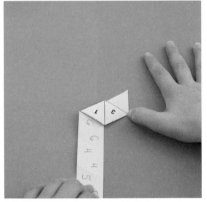

Fig. 5. Fold the first 5 to face the second 5.

project continues ▶

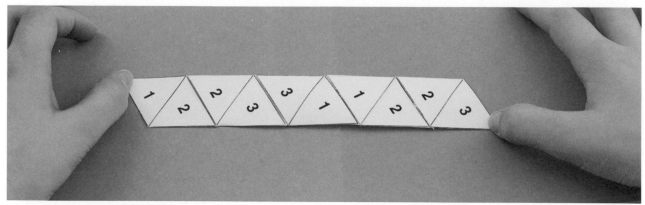

Fig. 6. Side 1: Front of the fully folded strip.

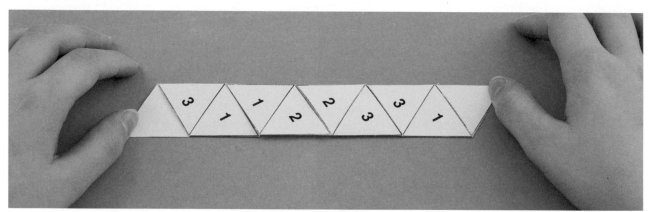

Fig. 7. Side 2: Back of the fully folded strip.

8 Keep going around until you have a straight strip of ten triangles. On one side it will read 1-2-2-3-3-1-1-2-2-3. On the other side, it will start with a blank triangle, then read 3-1-1-2-2-3-3-1 and then end with a blank triangle. *Fig. 6* and *Fig. 7.*

9 Hold the folded strip with side 1 face up so you see no blank triangles and have a 1 on the left. Fold the 3s that are next to each other (the fourth and fifth triangles from the left) together so you have four 2s visible next to each other. *Fig. 6* and *Fig. 8.*

10 Now fold the two visible 3s on top of each other. Fold so you can see all six 2s with the 3 on top. *Fig. 9* (on page 106).

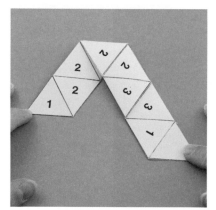

Fig. 8. Four 2s are adjacent to each other.

11 Tuck the newly visible 3 under the last 2 that is currently under that 3. *Fig. 10.*

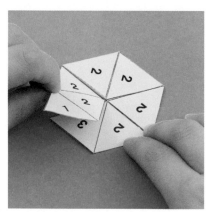

Fig. 10. Tuck 3 under 2.

12 You will now see all six 2s and have an extra triangle with a 1 sticking out. *Fig. 11.*

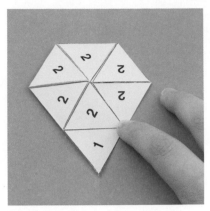

Fig. 11. All six 2s are visible with additional 1 sticking out.

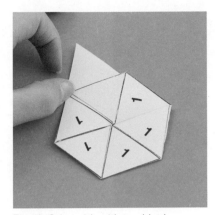

Fig. 12. Other side with two blank triangles.

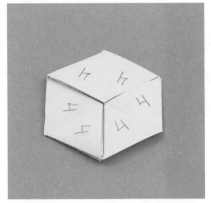

Fig. 13. One of the harder to find sides.

13 Flip the whole contraption over and you'll see two blank triangles. *Fig. 12.*

14 Glue the blank triangles together. You'll end up with all 1s on one side and all 2s on the other.

15 Try flexing the same way you flexed the trihexaflexagon. There are six sides, but some are easier to find than others. It took us a couple of minutes to find all six sides, so don't give up! If you can't find all six sides, try pushing in a different set of adjacent triangles instead. *Fig. 13.*

16 Decorate your hexahexaflexagon to make it even more interesting!

BONUS LEVEL

Trihexaflexagons have three faces and "tri" means "three." In this activity, you made a shape called a hexahexaflexagon because it has six faces, and "hex" means "six."

Look up directions on the Internet for how to make hexaflexagons with even more faces, square flexagons, and other interesting flexing shapes.

You can even make flexagons out of cloth or find patterns to knit or crochet them!

THE MATH IN THE FUN

The trihexaflexagon project in this book demonstrates a cyclic group of order three, meaning it has three elements you can get by cycling. The hexahexaflexagon has a more complicated, noncyclic structure. That's why some of the faces are easier to get to than others.

Hexaflexagons were invented by Arthur H. Stone, whose friend Richard Feynman created diagrams to track how to get from one face to another. Richard later became one of the most famous scientists in the world, even winning the Nobel Prize in physics. One of his big contributions to physics was the concept of a Feynman diagram to pictorially describe the behavior of subatomic particles. Those Feynman diagrams have nothing to do with the diagrams he made to track how to get from one face of a hexaflexagon to another.

Shing-Tung Yau

Born: April 4, 1949

INTELLECTUAL FAMILY

Shing-Tung Yau grew up in Hong Kong with seven siblings, one of whom became a mathematician as well! Shing-Tung began studying mathematics as soon as he could at the Chinese University of Hong Kong, later earning his PhD at the University of California, Berkeley, in the United States. Chiu Chen Ying, Shing-Tung's father, was a professor of Chinese philosophy and greatly encouraged his son to study Chinese literature and history. Shing-Tung eventually published the essay "On Mathematics and Chinese Literature," connecting the two.

DISTINGUISHED CAREER

Shing-Tung has held a number of distinguished positions and worked at many prestigious universities. He has spent the bulk of his career at Harvard University, where he has met and worked with many notable mathematicians, including Fan Chung, who is also featured in this book. Shing-Tung's teaching style is extremely hands-on. He holds seminars every day for his students, while most professors only hold them once a week. Shing-Tung's mathematical work has had far-reaching effects. A famous mathematician named William Thurston credited Shing-Tung with changing the entire direction of geometry research in just a few years. The existence theorem for Calabi-Yau manifolds is considered pivotal in modern string theory. His work is also relevant to general relativity, a key area of physics, engineering, and other applications of math.

STATELESS

Shing-Tung lived in the United States for a long time, which became a problem in 1978. He had lived in the United States for so long that he lost his Hong Kong resident status, even though he wasn't a citizen of the United States. This left Shing-Tung "stateless" for twelve years, meaning that he wasn't a citizen of any country! In fact, he was still stateless when he won the Fields Medal, the math equivalent of the Nobel Prize, which he mentioned proudly during his acceptance speech. He did eventually become a United States citizen.

PROMOTING MATH

Dr. Shing-Tung Yau works tirelessly to improve mathematical studies and opportunities in China. He pushed for donations to create outreach programs and conferences to spread the love and development of math. These included meetings for high school and college students, such as the "Why Math? Ask Masters!" panel in Hangzhou and the "Wonder of Mathematics" panel in Hong Kong. He cofounded a popular mathematics book series, "Mathematics and Mathematical People," and also set up the Hang Lung Award for high school students. Shing-Tung began his outreach at the Institute of Mathematical Sciences at the Chinese University of Hong Kong. Three years later, he created his own math center called the Morningside Centre of Mathematics in Beijing. He is still a director at both and at the Center of Mathematical Science at Zhejiang University! More recently, Shing-Tung turned his attention toward Taiwan, where he created the National Center of Theoretical Sciences. He is also the founding director of the Center of Mathematical Sciences and Applications at Harvard University, a multidisciplinary research center. And he has advised more than seventy PhD students!

AWARDS AND HONORS

Shing-Tung has won numerous honors and awards and published too many articles to count, but likely more than five hundred! He won a MacArthur Fellowship, which is commonly called the "genius prize." In addition to being a coauthor of many textbooks, he has written a few popular solo books. Shing-Tung certainly keeps himself busy!

ALIEN CITY

Shing-Tung Yau and Fan Chung met while combining ideas from separate areas of math to make new and interesting discoveries. We will put together many of our previous projects to create a beautiful alien city on which we can play a game!

MATERIALS

- Large piece or pieces of cardboard adding up to at least 2 by 2 feet (61 by 61 cm)
- Paint and paintbrush
- Square-wheeled car and road from earlier in this book
- Three-dimensional shapes from nets earlier in this book
- Hexaflexagons from earlier in the book
- Fibonacci spiral from earlier in the book (optional)
- At least half a dozen dice, preferably in different shapes
- Ruler
- String
- Scissors
- 2 tokens
- A six-sided die

Fig. 7. Completed city!

DIRECTIONS

MAKE THE BASE

1 First, we will make the base of our alien planet. For this you will need one or more large pieces of cardboard. We chose two medium squares and one large one, but you can pick different shapes if you like. Make sure there is a large center area on your planet, large enough to hold the track for your square-wheeled car. Paint your cardboard whatever color you like. This will be the natural color of your planet. We chose Mars red. *Fig. 1* and *Fig. 2*.

2 Place your square-wheeled car and road in the middle of the city base, separating two sides of the city so there is room to put buildings on either side of the road. Feel free to paint your road and car. *Fig. 3*.

3 Take several of the three-dimensional nets you made earlier and place them throughout your city. These are your buildings. Feel free to add other interesting geometric shapes from projects from this book or that you find around your house too. *Fig. 4*.

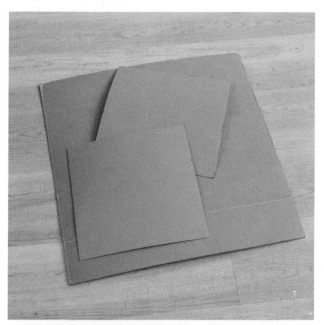

Fig. 1. Large pieces of cardboard.

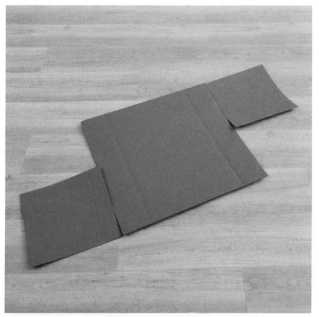

Fig. 2. Painted cardboard.

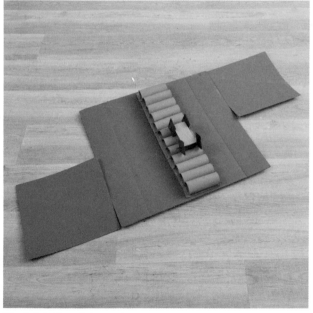

Fig. 3. Add the city's road.

Fig. 4. Add buildings.

project continues ▶

FINAL PROJECT

Fig. 5. Add hexaflexagons.

Fig. 6. Add sidewalks.

4 Place some hexaflexagons on or around your buildings to serve as spaceships. *Fig. 5.*

5 Add some flat (not folded) nets as sidewalk decorations for your planet. *Fig. 6.*

6 If desired, put a Fibonacci spiral in the city to represent a garden or sculpture.

7 Finally, place the dice around your city. These are the geometric citizens of your new world. *Fig. 7.*

SET UP THE GAME

1 Measure and cut a piece of string 1 inch (2.5 cm) long.

2 Measure and cut a piece of string 2 inches (5.1 cm) long.

3 Repeat for 3, 4, 5, and 6 inches (7.6, 10.2, 12.7, 15.2 cm). *Fig. 8.*

4 Take all of the aliens (dice) out of your city except for two. Place these two remaining dice as far away from each other in your city as you can. The most important thing is that the aliens are on opposite sides of the road.

Fig. 8. Cut six strings.

RULES OF THE GAME

1 The goal of this game is to get your aliens together so they can hang out. To do this, the two players each take turns rolling a six-sided die.

2 When you roll a die, you get to move your alien up to that many inches. Use the strings to help you measure.

EXAMPLE: If you roll a 4, use the string that is 4 inches (10.2 cm) long.

3 Put one end of the string on the alien and the other end in the direction you want to go. Then move the alien toward the empty end. You can always choose to stop early. You can also use one move to go in multiple directions. For example, you might go 1 inch (2.5 cm) forward, then turn and move 3 inches (7.6 cm) in a different direction. *Fig. 9.*

4 The aliens cannot move through buildings, so you'll have to find a way around them.

5 After moving your alien, the other player takes a turn.

6 Continue to alternate until you reach each other.

SPECIAL RULE: Aliens cannot cross the road. That would be dangerous! Instead, when they are next to the road—that means touching it—you can use your moves to roll the car that many humps in the road (toilet paper rolls) in any direction you want. When the car is next to your alien, you can use your move to walk onto the car or across it to get to the other side of the road. Bonus points if your aliens meet in the car!

Fig. 9. Measure using the strings.

BONUS LEVEL

Congratulations, you have created your very own city out of a variety of mathematical projects! Try to incorporate other math projects to expand your city! You can also play the game with more aliens. Just start them far away from each other. Alternatively, you can have them all start at the same place and race to a building or location of your choice! There are so many games you can play and create with your city!

THE MATH IN THE FUN

In math, different areas and discoveries often work together to form new and wonderful combinations! As we mentioned at the beginning of this book, math is a big, beautiful tree with endless and often connected and overlapping branches. In this project, we put many different kinds of math together to create a new game and an entire universe! If we could do that with just a book, imagine what mathematicians like you can accomplish if they work together!

HINTS AND SOLUTIONS

BUILDING BUILDINGS

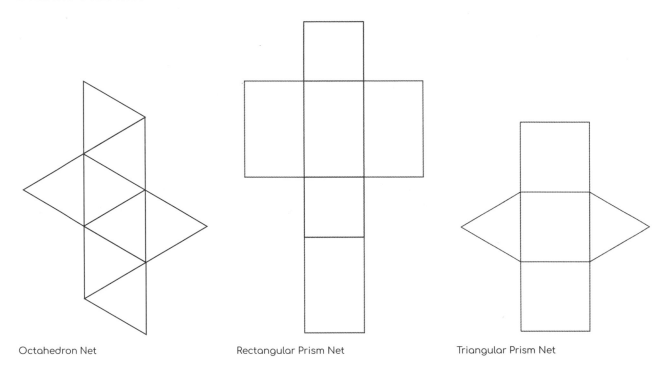

Octahedron Net

Rectangular Prism Net

Triangular Prism Net

MANCALA

We double the extra number of seeds because we need the extra to fill up the missing amount on the other side. We need twice this number, however, to know how much the player won by because before they can fill in the missing number for the other player, they have to fill in their own.

So why is the number a player won by always even? Well, the total number of seeds in the game is an even number, so when you add up the seeds each player has in their bank at the end, it must be an even number. Two numbers add to an even number if they are both odd or both even. Similarly, an even number minus an even number is an even number, and an odd number minus an odd number is an even number. Using this logic, either both players had an odd number of seeds at the end of the game and thus the difference is even. Or they both had an even number and the difference is still even. Therefore, the number of seeds a player wins by must be even!

BINARY BRACELET

We don't need to use delimiters because the code for each letter has exactly seven 0s or 1s. So we know a new letter starts after seven 0s and 1s.

Look at the codes for a few matching uppercase and lowercase letters. What is the same? What is different?

- Every letter starts with a 1.

- Uppercase letters have a 0 next.

- Lowercase letters have a 1 next.

- The last four digits of each uppercase and lowercase letter match.

The secret message is: Math is fun.

CURVE STITCHING

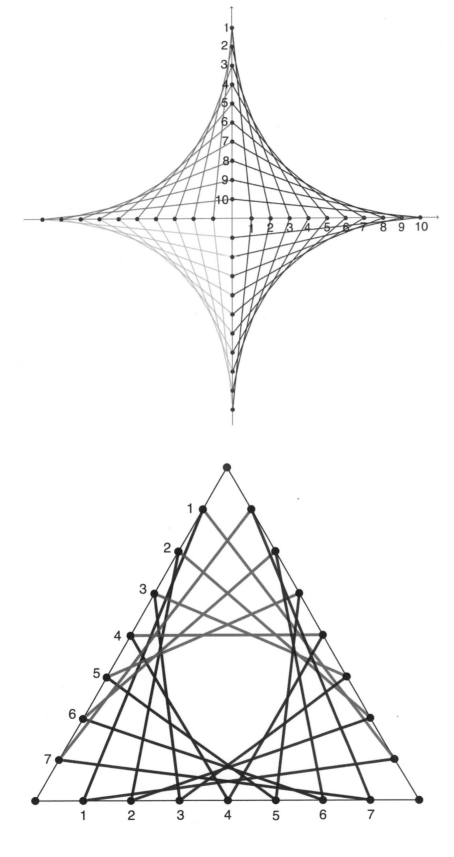

The princess asks one brother, "Is that one older than the other?" This question guarantees she will get either the oldest or the youngest. Why?

If she asks the oldest brother whether the first one she points to is older than the other, he will say yes if she pointed at the middle one first, and no if she pointed at the youngest first. If he says no, she should choose the one she pointed to first. If he says yes, she should choose the one she pointed to second.

If she asks the youngest brother whether the first one she pointed to is younger than the second, he will say no if she pointed to the older one, and yes if she pointed to the middle one first. If he says yes, she should pick the one she pointed to second, and if he says no she should pick the one she pointed to first.

Either way, if the prince says yes, she should pick the one she pointed to second and if he says no, she should pick the one she pointed to first. This guarantees she doesn't end up with the middle brother.

Why does this work? Why do we pick the one we pointed to first when we hear the answer no and the other when given the answer yes? See if you can figure it out!

NOTE: If she asked the question of the middle brother, she won't know which is which, but because she never picks the prince she questions, she'll end up with the oldest or the youngest anyway!

In the end, the princess realizes the best lab partner was sitting in front of her the whole time. She and the other princess partner up and both of them are truthful all the time.

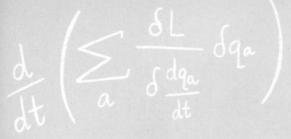

GLOSSARY

Axiom: A math statement that is assumed to be true and from which other math ideas follow.

Bar graph: A visual presentation of data shown through differences in the height of the bars.

Binary codes: Codes using only Os and 1s.

Bits: The smallest possible unit of information in a code.

Butterfly effect: The idea that one small change can have drastic effects on an outcome.

Categorical data: Data of groups.

Catenary curve: The curve a theoretical perfect chain would make when only supported at its ends.

Convex: A shape whose surface curves outward (such as a sphere).

Deficit: Having less than none of a resource, owing someone that resource.

Delimiter: Something that marks the beginning or end of a piece of data.

Edge: The connection between two vertices in a three-dimensional shape.

Equilateral triangle: A triangle where all sides are the same length.

Face: A side of a three-dimensional shape.

Fibonacci sequence: A sequence of numbers where the next number is found by adding the previous two numbers in the sequence. The sequence starts with two 1s.

Hyperbola: Intersection of a plane and a cone (if you cut a cone, the shape of the cut).

Hyperboloid: A three-dimensional shape similar to an hourglass.

Mathemagician: A mathematical magician.

Net: The outside of a three-dimensional shape when flattened.

Octahedron: An eight-sided three-dimensional shape whose faces are triangles.

Pie chart: A visual presentation of data by wedges in a circle.

Pigeonhole principle: If every pigeon must go into a hole, and there are more pigeons than holes, then at least two pigeons will have to share a hole.

Pyramid: A three-dimensional shape made up of triangles on top of a base. Pyramids are named by the shape of their base.

Rectangular prism: A three-dimensional shape whose six faces are rectangles.

Regular tetrahedron: A four-sided three-dimensional shape where all faces are the same size equilateral triangle.

Riffle shuffle: A standard way of shuffling a deck of cards.

Sphere: The word mathematicians use for a perfectly round ball.

Square pyramid: A pyramid with a square base.

Surplus: Having extra of a resource.

Tessellation/tiling: A group of tiles filling a plane.

Tile: A shape with no holes that can tile the plane.

Tile the plane: A shape can tile the plane if you can use many copies of it to cover a flat surface without gaps or overlaps.

Torus: The shape of a doughnut or bagel.

Translating: When you translate a shape, you move it into a different position but make no changes to the shape.

Triangular prism: A three-dimensional shape whose ends have the same size and shape triangles and whose other faces are rectangles.

Triangular pyramid: A pyramid with a triangular base.

Vertices: The corners of three-dimensional shapes.

PULLOUTS AND TEMPLATES

HYPERBOLIC SLOT TEMPLATE

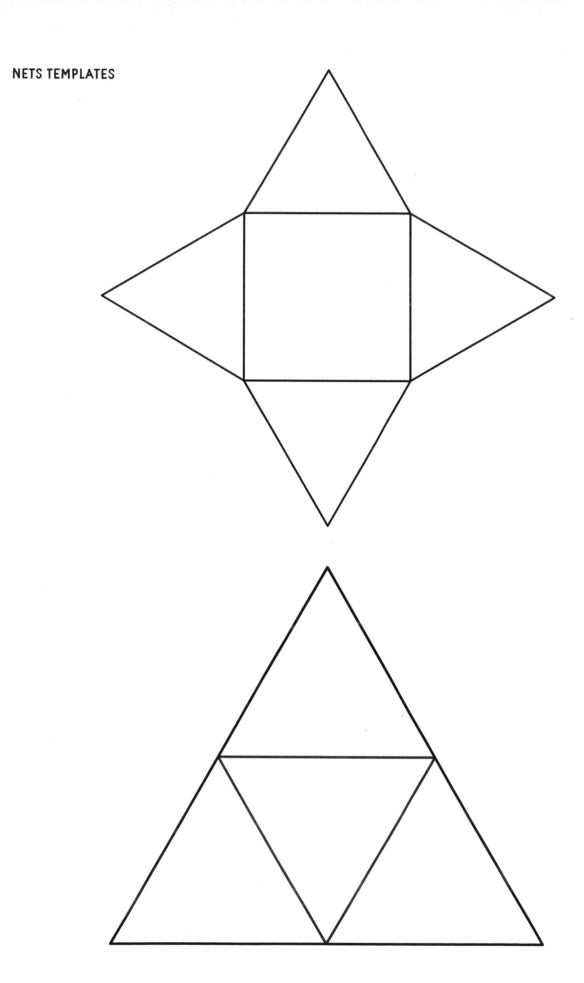

Pizza Pie Chart

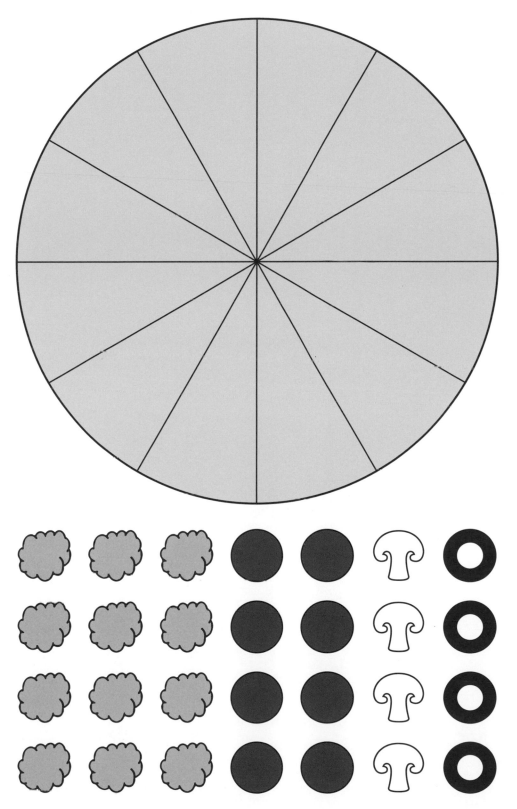

Trihexaflexagon Template

Hexahexaflexagon Template

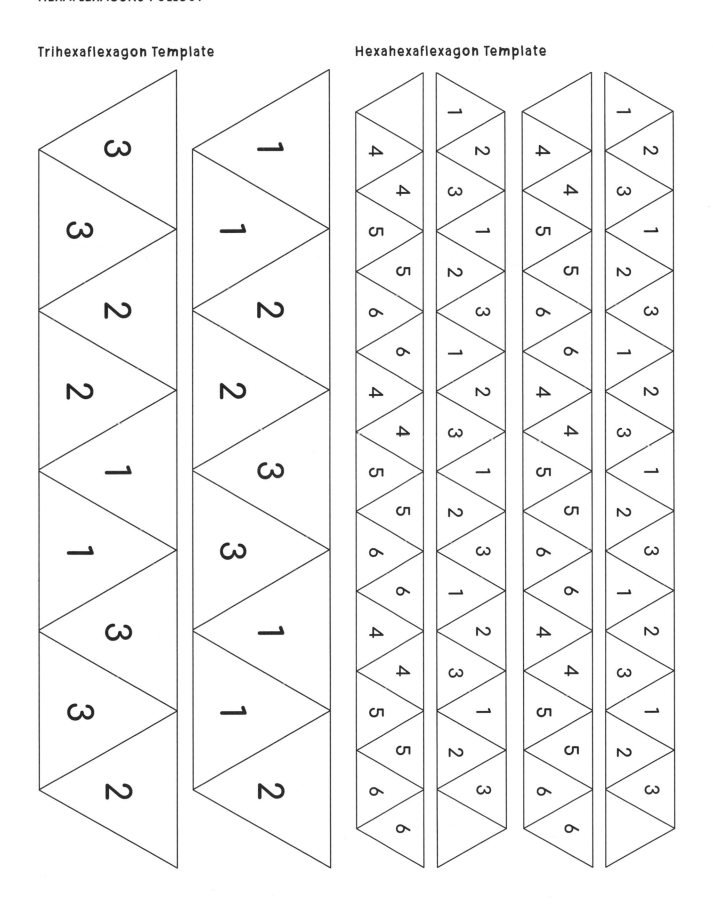

ACKNOWLEDGMENTS

We would like to thank Ron Rapoport, Jasper Rosenberg, Elliot Marks, and Jenise Aminoff for their extremely thorough comments.

Of course we thank our editor, Jonathan Simcosky, for his guidance; Joy Acquilo, who believed in the book; and Liz Heinecke, who was kind enough to let us add to the wonderful series of books she created.

From day one, we wanted Kelly Anne Dalton to be our illustrator. We are blown away by her talent and ability to subtly include details from the biographies into her work.

Thank you so much to Heather Godin, art director extraordinaire, who was irreplaceable in helping us achieve our vision, and to Glenn Scott, a true pro in capturing even the smallest of details with his camera. M. Godin provided the super cute artwork for the turtle and dog tessellations, and J. Yoder created the awesome elephant tessellations. We also thank Zack Chung for sharing his thoughts on dyslexic-friendly fonts.

We also thank Fan Chung for providing fun stories about Yau and other insight into many of today's mathematicians.

And of course, we thank all the kids whose smiling faces light up this book and their parents for bringing them to us, especially with the added challenges of the COVID-19 pandemic.

$$\sqrt{1 + 2\sqrt{1 + 3\sqrt{1 + \cdots}}}$$

ABOUT THE AUTHORS

Rebecca Rapoport is the author of *Math Games Lab for Kids*, a book of fun and engaging, hands-on math activities for elementary school students to enjoy with an adult helper or for middle school students to savor on their own.

Rapoport has also been writing *Your Daily Epsilon of Math*, a math snack per day wall calendar for adults, for the past several years. Each month features a stunning math image and an intellectual challenge for every day of the month.

Rapoport holds degrees in mathematics from Harvard and Michigan State. From her first job out of college, as one of the pioneers of Harvard's Internet education offerings, she has been passionate about encouraging her love of math in others. As an early contributor to both retail giant Amazon.com and Akamai Technologies, the number one firm in cloud computing, Rapoport played a key role in several elements of the Internet revolution.

Rapoport returned to her first love, education, as an innovator of new methods to introduce children and adults to the critically important world of STEM as COO of an enrichment center dedicated to helping kids explore the creative side of science, technology, engineering, art, and math. Currently, Rapoport is a full-time math evangelist.

Allanna Chung is an aspiring screenwriter with a deep passion for math. One of her favorite pastimes is showing just how fun and beautiful math can be to those who have learned to dislike it. She works as a teacher of STEM and as a personal tutor to help students learn math in ways that work for them.

ABOUT THE PHOTOGRAPHER

Glenn Scott has been creating images at his GSP studio in the downtown Arts District in Beverly, Massachusetts, for more than twenty-five years. His favorite projects feature simple subjects complemented by inventive surroundings. Enjoy Glenn's portfolio at glennscottphotography.com.

ABOUT THE ILLUSTRATOR

Kelly Anne Dalton is an artist, illustrator, and storyteller living in the wild mountains of Montana. Her elegant and enchanting work can be found on everything from board books to middle grade novel covers, home decor and gift products, and stationery lines. When not drawing, daydreaming, and creating new stories and characters, Kelly Anne can be found trail running in the forests near her home.